EDUCATION AMONG SCHEDULED TRIBES

MR. KRITTIBAS DATTA DR. MUKTA GOYAL

Made with ♥ on the Notion Press Platform
www.notionpress.com

Contents

Preface

The Tribal population in India is considered to be the oldest population and has been living for centuries in the forest and hilly regions. India has the single largest tribal population in the world. Tribal communities in India have been historically deprived of access to resources and opportunities, including the opportunity to get educated. For such historically deprived communities, providing access to education is simply not enough, the government has to take a proactive role in creating overall conditions and opportunities that will facilitate their transition and breaking of the intergenerational cycle of poverty and illiteracy. Education is an important parameter of development as an individual society. After the seven diced of independence, the tribal groups are facing many challenging issues in their daily life. Without the development of the educational status, Indian tribes cannot be able to overcome the challenging factors. Education for all (EFA) is an international commitment to ensure that every child receives basic education of good quality. In India education for all has been given but it is fact that tribal children are deprived of to access education at present.

Our constitution laid down numerous provisions for the uplift of tribal communities but still, they are confronted with various challenges. Despite several initiatives that have been taken by the Government to enhance educational status ever since independence, the literacy rate among Schedule Tribes has remained low. The literacy rate is not satisfactory for the Indian tribes, besides the dropout and stagnation among the tribals are alarming. Many times, the government reports mentioning a lot of obstacles to tribal education in India that make more challenges to the education of the tribals. After independence, our government has taken many initiatives to develop tribal education, but today we are unable to say that tribal education in India is sustainable conditions. But the educational stats of the tribal people have indeed grown up day by day with the government and semi-governmental initiatives. So, without the development of the educational status of the tribals cannot be reached a sustainable development of the tribes. The present volume focused on education among scheduled tribes in India from different viewpoints.

This work is possible with the blessing of our parents and family members whose continued inspiration guided us to publish this book in time. As a whole, the book got the complete shape because of the great initiative of the Notion press. We would like to express our thanks to all the parts of the publishing house.

Krittibas Datta
Dr. Mukta Goyal

CHAPTER ONE

EVOLUTION OF TRIBAL INDIA: THE PRE-INDEPENDENCE ERA

Introduction

India being a multi-racial, multi-lingual and multi-strict country, it shouldn't shock us with the way that Indian culture isn't homogenous. The ancestral gatherings, who live in enormous or little fixations amidst timberlands or in regions which were to a great extent distant till late times, involve a conspicuous spot among such gatherings. They are pleased with their social legacy and lead a particular lifestyle. The English way to deal with ancestral society was essentially administered by provincial personal circumstance. The tribesmen were by and large permitted to seek after their life in disengagement somewhat on the grounds that the undertaking of controlling the peripheral regions where they resided was troublesome and somewhat in light of the fact that many officials truly had the point of view that these individuals were improved left as they were. The point was to keep up with business as usual. This empowered the personal stakes viz., the zamindars, property managers, project workers and cash banks, to take advantage of and usurp the ancestral terrains and timberlands.

The tribesmen needed to stay helpless before authorities and usurers. Their infringement onancestral land and property prompted the episode of a progression of uprisings. One more gathering that attempted to being the tribals under their impact were the Christian Ministers. They utilized assorted systems to spread the message of the gospel among them. The public authority anyway wondered whether or not to meddle at whatever point any indication of unsent among the ancestral populace rose to the top. In some cases through rough enslavement and very frequently through dealings with clan leaders and the more remarkable areas of ancestral society, they prevailed with regards to determining extraordinary political benefit. 'The central point of the organization was to get harmony. They were not worried about ancestral advancement in a way. Review settlements were completed and income gathered any place and whenever the situation allows India is renowned for the adivasi or tribal people who live there. The term "adivasi" denotes that they were the lands earliest or original occupants and that they were native to the soil and their natural habitat. Tribes are typically thought of as simple social groups whose members cooperate for a common goal, such as welfare, and speak a same dialect. Tribes have a set habitat and territory, and their social organisation is built mostly on family links, cultural homogeneity, a shared conception of the gods and ancestors, as well as a shared dialect and folklore. In addition to giving them a sense of independence, self-identity, and respect, their environment and culture also give them the ability to stand together against any form of exploitation, oppression, or harassment by outsiders like zamindars, monarchs, British, and others.

The Tribes have developed a complex custodial way of life over the years. Tribes are a part of their territories, which are what make them who they are. In the past, the Tribes effectively functioned as independent "first nations." They were considered to be a part of the "unknown frontier" during the pre-colonial era, where the rule of the king actually did not reach. Tribes made their own rules independent of the particular king. The interaction between mainstream communities and indigenous tribes was altered by the arrival of Europeans and the following colonisation. Since ancient times, tribes in India have been shielded from the effects of attacks by foreign invaders, encroachments, wars, and other issues that affect mainstream civilization. Due to their remoteness, they lag behind their neighbouring communities in terms of socialisation, culture, and education. Since they were not seen as a danger to their kingdoms, local monarchs frequently had minimal interactions with them. Even though the rulers were aware of the terrible situations the tribes were in, they were in a bad position to act. Until the arrival of the British, this non-interventionist policy was maintained without interruption. The British established a straightforward system of managing the tribal areas under their colonial reign. When the British arrived, they brought with them many changes to their way of life as well as strangers into their domain.

As a result, they were demoted from being landowners to being slaves and debts. Essentially, the uprisings were a defence of their independence and a reaction to this unwanted encroachment. Different models of tribal development:

The ways to deal with the advancement of the ancestral individuals in India can, be partitioned into three classifications, for example, 1. Noninterventionist Approach, 2. Osmosis Approach, and 3. Mix Approach

- **Independent Methodology:**

It was trailed by the English after the strategies of the English prompted rebels against them by the Clans. It appeared as English assigning ancestral regions as 'barred regions ' in light of the rule of non-impedance

Under English rule, the expansion of a unified organization over regions, which recently were outside the viable control of royal rulers, denied numerous native clans of their independence.

However English managers in no way wanted to slow down tribesmen's freedoms and conventional way of living, the actual course of foundation of the rule of law in distant regions presented the clans to the tension of further developed populaces.

The regions which had recently been practically un-managed have been risky for outcasts who didn't partake in the certainty and altruism of the ancestral occupants, merchants and cash loan specialists could now sccure themselves under the assurance of the English organization and generally speaking they were trailed by pilgrims who prevailed with regards to getting huge stretches of clans' territory.

Managerial officials who didn't comprehend ancestral arrangement of land residency presented uniform techniques for income assortment. In any case, these had the un-expected impact of working with the estrangement of ancestral land to individuals from cutting edge populaces.

There were a few clans, in any case, who defied an organization, which permitted untouchables to deny them of their territory.

In the Chhota Nagpur and the Santhal Parganas such uprisings of frantic tribesmen repeated all through the nineteenth 100 years, and there were minor risings in the Organization plots of Madras and in a portion of the locale of Bombay occupied by Bhils.

Santhals are accepted to have lost around 10,000 men in their defiance of 1855. These insurgences were not generally pointed principally at the

English organization, yet they were a response to their double-dealing and persecution by Hindu landowners and cash moneylenders.

Now and again these uprisings prompted official requests and to administrative institutions pointed toward safeguarding clans' on the whole correct to their territory. Seen in verifiable point of view apparently land estrangement regulations had, in general, just a palliative impact. In many regions infringement ashore held by clans proceeded with even notwithstanding defensive regulation.

- **Absorption Approach**

This had confidence in standard Tribals and their way of life totally disintegrating their way of life totally by causing them to acknowledge the standard culture

Acknowledgment or refusal of the need for digestion with Hindu society is at last an issue of values. Before, Hindu society had been lenient toward bunches that wouldn't adjust to the guidelines set by the higher stations.

Those gatherings were denied equivalent custom status; yet no endeavors were made to redirect them from their picked way of living. Lately this disposition has changed.

It is the impact of the Western confidence in widespread qualities which has energized a feeling of narrow mindedness opposite social and social divergences.

India is a multilingual, a multiracial nation and multi-social. What's more, the same length as the minorities are allowed to follow their customary lifestyle, apparently not out of the question that the way of life and the social request of clans anyway particular from that of the larger part local area ought to likewise be regarded.

Absorption will happen naturally and unavoidably where little ancestral gatherings are encased inside mathematically more grounded Hindu populaces.

In India's northern and north-eastern wilderness live enthusiastic ancestral populaces which oppose digestion as well as consideration inside Hindu position framework.

- **Incorporation approach**

The Public authority of India has embraced a strategy of combination of tribals with the standard targeting fostering an inventive change between the clans and non clans prompting a mindful organization.

By taking on the approach of combination or moderate assimilation the Public authority has established the groundwork for the uninhibited walk of the tribals towards fairness, up versatility, and financial practicality and guaranteed vicinity to the public standard.

The constitution has committed the country to two blueprints in regard of planned clans, viz.

Giving assurance to their particular lifestyle.

Shielding them from social foul play and all types of double-dealing and segregation and carrying them at standard with the remainder of the country so they might be incorporated with the public life.

In this way by the Constitution Request 1950 gave by the Leader of India in exercise of abilities presented by Clause9 (I) of Article 342 of the Constitution of India 255 clans in 17 states were proclaimed to be planned clans.

India's arrangement at the hour of autonomy and Ancestral Panchasheel:

The Constitution through a few Articles has accommodated the financial turn of events and strengthening of Planned Clans. Yet, there has been no public strategy, which might have made an interpretation of the sacred arrangements into a reality. Five standards spelt out in 1952, known as Nehruvian Panchasheel, have been directing the organization of ancestral issues.

Jawaharlal Nehru trusted that the inspire of the ancestral needed to happen through a sluggish course of their modernization, even while their way of life must be safeguarded. He had figured out the accompanying five standards for the strategy to be sought after versus the tribals. They are:

- Tribals ought to be permitted to create as indicated by their own virtuoso.
- Tribals' privileges in land and backwoods ought to be regarded.
- Ancestral groups ought to be prepared to embrace organization and improvement without an excessive number of pariahs being drafted.
- Ancestral advancement ought to be embraced without upsetting ancestral social and social establishments.

- The file of ancestral advancement ought to be a mind-blowing nature and not the cash spent.

Understanding that the Nehruvian Panchasheel was long on sweeping statements and short on particulars, the Public authority of India framed a Service of Ancestral Issues without precedent for October 1999 to speed up ancestral turn of events.

Tribal Administration in Pre-Independence

Due to the tribal people's generally inaccessible environments, such as distant hills, marshy or malaria-infested jungles, and hostile areas, contact between British officials and the tribal people remained challenging during the period of British control. The British relied on information from Christian missionaries and had a "leave them alone" approach. Instead of concentrating their authority on smaller tribal groups, they aimed to control the majority of the Indian population that was easily accessible. As a result, they continued to keep the indigenous people apart from the rest of the nation. They made little effort to free them from the influence of missionaries, the grasp of moneylenders, landowners, and contractors.

For the advantage of the class of people who were ardent supporters of British dominance in India, Lord Cornwallis established a system of land tenure in India in 1793. The government demanded rent payments from zamindars under the new land tenure system, which recognised them as landowners. As a result, zamindars could use land as both private property and a marketable good. With this method, the land was divided into small parts and given to several feudal lords. The tribals were quite upset about this new land tenure structure. These factors contributed to the unrest:

- The indigenous people's traditional economy was put in jeopardy, and they lost their claim to agricultural areas. The British government passed the first tenant law in 1859 to try and solve the issue, but it had no effect on helping tribal people and poor peasants.
- To keep tribes from fighting with established farmers, retired army personnel were permitted to settle on the outskirts of some tribal districts. As a result, tribal people developed a gulf of mistrust and suspicion toward the nearby non-tribals as a result of colonial policy.
- Forests, which are essential for obtaining sustainable means of subsistence, were now protected. The majority of tribal communities collect fuel, fodder, medicinal plants, roots, tubers, vegetable leaves, and

other items from forests in order to survive. An important supply of protein is obtained through wild game hunting.

- The conservation of natural forests led to restrictions on shifting farming. Without giving the tribes alternative means of subsistence, this restricted their tribal rights to the forests. The British government created the First Forest Policy of 1894, a policy on forest reservation, to limit environmental exploitation. In many ways, it changed the tribal way of life. Formerly controlled by tribal groups, the forests gradually came under the administration of the Forest Department. Their historical right to the forest was no longer acknowledged, and they were no longer free to travel around the forest as they pleased. Tribes were forced out of their natural home, which led to them turning to criminal activity. Such tribes were subsequently classified as criminal tribes by the British authority.
- Incentives for native art and crafts were also withheld, which gave the tribes the impression that their goods fell short of expectations.
- Numerous tribe members were hired at minimum salary by mining and steel firms as a result of modernization. They had to take out loans to make ends meet. As payment for their obligations, the moneylenders instituted forced and bonded labour.

Important Tribal Uprising in 18th and 19th Century

The following are a few of the most significant tribal uprisings from the 18th and 19th centuries:

- **Rangpur, Bengal, Peasant Uprising (1783 AD)**

- The British began utilising revenue contracts to extort as much money as they could from peasants after capturing control of Bengal in 1757 AD.
- The peasants turned to the courts after the executives did little to address their complaints.
- Under the direction of Dirjinarain, they attacked the agricultural storage facilities and cutcheries owned by contractors or public authorities.
- Muslims and Hindus fought side by side throughout the uprising. The company's military staff eventually took charge of the situation and put a stop to the uprising.

- **Kol Rebellion in 1832**

- Among the tribes that inhabited Chhotanagpur and its environs were the Kols.
- Under their local leaders, they had full control, but when the British came, everything changed.
- Along with the British, traders and moneylenders arrived.
- The Kol family was consequently compelled to sell their property to foreign farmers and to face a hefty tax burden. As a result, many people ended up working as bonded labour.
- The British legal practises also infuriated the Kols.
- The Kols organised an uprising against the British and moneylenders from 1831 to 1832.
- They burned down houses while murdering several strangers. This bloody conflict continued for two years before the British utilised superior armaments to ruthlessly suppress it.
- It took troops from Benares and Calcutta to quell the Kol Revolt because it was so ferocious.

- **The Munda Ulgulan**

- The Mundas lived at Chotanagar.
- The Khunt Katti structure, a system of land sharing, was employed by the Mundas. After the British arrived, the Zamindari system took the place of the Khunkatti organisation. The tribal members were forced to labour, which resulted to debt.
- In the late 18th and early 19th centuries, there were a number of revolts against the British.
- An uprising was declared in 1894 by the charismatic and successful commander Birsa Munda.
- He has a public rebellion against the government planned. He encouraged others to skip paying their debts and taxes.
- Before his parole in 1897, he was apprehended and sentenced to two years in prison.
- In December 1899, he launched an armed uprising against the government and landowners.
- The Mundas burned down churches, mansions of landowners, government buildings, and other property owned by the British.
- In 1900, Birsa Munda had been captured. He passed away from cholera in prison at the age of barely 25.

Tribal Panchasheel and Indian policy at independence

The Constitution includes provisions for the socioeconomic advancement and self-determination of Scheduled Tribes in a number of its Articles. However, there hasn't been any national policy to assist make the constitutional requirements a reality. The management of tribal affairs has been governed by the Nehruvian Panchasheel, a set of five tenets outlined in 1952.

Jawaharlal Nehru thought that the development of the tribal people needed to happen through a gradual modernisation process, even while their culture needed to be preserved. For the tribal policy to be followed, he had developed the following five principles. As follows:

1. It is best to let tribes flourish at their own unique pace.
2. The land and forest rights of tribes should be honoured.
3. Without over-involving outsiders, tribal teams should be trained to handle administration and development.
4. It is important to pursue tribal development without upsetting tribal social and cultural structures.
5. The standard of their lives, not the amount of money invested, should be used to measure tribal development.

In order to hasten tribal development, the Indian government established a Ministry of Tribal Affairs for the first time in October 1999 after realising that the Nehruvian Panchasheel was long on generalities and short on specifics.

The Draft National Policy on Tribes has recently been released by the Ministry of Tribal Affairs. The Ministry will finalise the policy in light of input from tribal leaders, the concerned States, people, businesses in the public and private sectors, and NGOs. The National Policy is aware of:

1. The majority of Scheduled Tribes still experience poverty.
2. Their rates of literacy are low.
3. They experience sickness and undernourishment.
4. They are susceptible to being uprooted.

Additionally, it recognises that Scheduled Tribes as a whole serve as a repository for some indigenous knowledge and wisdom.

Recommendations and Findings

- The main reasons for each of these tribal uprisings in the 18th and 19th centuries were the quick changes made by the British to the economy, the government, and the land income structure. These changes upended the agrarian community, causing extreme and protracted suffering among its citizens.
- Tribal populations were horribly exploited after the British introduced moneylenders to them. The indigenous people were forced to work as labourers as a result of the newly established economic framework.
- The concept of exclusive ownership has replaced the common land ownership system that formerly existed in tribal societies.
- Utilization restrictions applied to hunting methods, shifting agriculture, and the use of forest products. The tribal people consequently lost their means of subsistence.
- In contrast to orthodox culture, which was characterised by class and status disparities, tribal life was often egalitarian. Tribals were demoted to the lowest levels of society when immigrants arrived.
- The very act of establishing law and order in remote locations exposed the tribes to pressure from more developed communities, even though British officials had no intention of interfering with tribesmen's rights and traditional way of life.
- Trading and moneylenders could now establish themselves under the protection of the British administration in the areas that had previously been essentially unadministered and unsafe for outsiders who did not enjoy the confidence and goodwill of the tribal inhabitants.

Conclusion

Since the arrival of the British till the present, administration in tribal areas has seen significant changes in the life of tribes, from total isolation to acculturation, assimilation, and incorporation into society. Contractors, bankers, businessmen, and other outsiders took advantage of tribes as a result of the colonial policy of "leave them alone." As a result, there was restlessness among the indigenous people, which gave rise to various movements. As a result, the tribal administration underwent a great deal of change, and new laws were created for the tribes' protection and advancement. With a few minor alterations, India continued to operate administratively in the same manner as the colonial powers after independence. Later on, however, tribal unity was viewed as the best course of action for the overall growth of the tribes.

CHAPTER TWO

EDUCATION STATUS OF TRIBAL POPULATION IN INDIA

Introduction

It cannot be overstated that education is one of the most effective ways to promote socioeconomic development among scheduled tribes.

People should encourage themselves in accordance with their talents and refrain from imposing anything on them. We should make an effort to support people's traditional expressions and cultures from the inside out... We should make an effort to organise and grow their very own group of people to complete tasks created by advancement and organisation. It's likely that some specialised workers from outside may be needed, especially at first. But we should endeavour to avoid bringing so many outcasts into our ancestral lands... Not by ideas or how much money was spent, but rather by the nature of the human being that is developed.

The native clans of India are the most seasoned occupants of the country. For centuries, ancestral social orders have been enslaved by additional as of late shown up gatherings; their property was removed, they were driven further into the bumpy crevasses and wilds, and they had to work for their oppressors frequently without installment. Today ancestral gatherings, which number in excess of 40 million, require exceptional consideration from the public authority despite the fact that they live generally detached from the public culture.

Before, numerous tribal gatherings had to absorb into the predominant culture of the country. However, a few gatherings, like the Bhils, Gonds, Santals, Oraons, Mundas, Khonds, Mizos, Nagas, and Khasis opposed change and osmosis to keep up with their social personalities and dialects. As per numerous Indians, their proceeded with disconnection presents issues to public coordination. Under the pennant of public solidarity, the public authority is currently bringing these minority bunches into the public standard. The principal question is whether ancestral social orders can enter the public standard while saving their unmistakable social, social and political convictions.People who prefer to live alone in a closed society and who have common origins and culture are said to belong to a tribe. Indian tribes are the indigenous or native people who live all throughout the nation.

The Indian population is largely made up of tribes, and tribal culture is a vital component of our intangible national heritage. As a result, we need to be aware of some of India's most significant tribes.

On the Indian subcontinent's mainland, there are pockets of tribal people in almost every state and union territory. Mizoram (94.4 percent of the population), Lakshadweep (94 percent), Meghalaya (86.1 percent), and Nagaland are the locations with the highest percentage of tribal settlements (86.5 percent). There are significant tribal settlements in Madhya Pradesh, Orissa, Maharashtra, Rajasthan, Chhattisgarh, Assam, and West Bengal as well. In a larger sense, 8.6% of India's population belongs to the scheduled tribes.

The Indian Tribes

The Gonds, Bhils (or Bheels), Katkari, Tharu, and The Great Andamanese Tribes are the most well-known tribes in India.

BHIL/BHEEL TRIBE

According to the 2011 census, the Bhil tribal group is the largest tribe in India out of all of these tribes. It makes up an astounding 38% of all scheduled indigenous people in the nation.

Although the Bhils have a language named after them, the majority of them also speak Marathi, Gujarati, and the language of the state in which they are headquartered. The tribe is the largest in India and has origins in Maharashtra, Chhattisgarh, portions of Gujarat, Rajasthan, and even some of Tripura.

In addition, Bhil is one of the relatively few scheduled tribes in India known for its distinctive kind of art, known as Bhil Art. These works of art are meant to depict the tribe members' daily lives. They use natural colour pigments generated from various leaves and flowers along with Neem tree twigs and branches as brushes to create a variety of objects.

The deities and ancestors are portrayed in Bhil art in the form of dots painted over the background of the artwork in various colours and patterns, giving it a distinctive appearance.

The Gonds of Andhra Pradesh

India's largest tribal community, the Gond, has a population of around 12 million. The Gond speak a subset of the Dravidian language family found in South Central called the Gondi-Manda. Incompatible theories on their genesis are entertained by linguists, ethnographers, and anthropologists. Due to the inadequate resolution of the genetic data or the small number of samples, genetic investigations of these individuals have thus far suffered. We have therefore used high-resolution data to examine four geographically distinct Gond groups in order to acquire a more complete understanding of the ancient origins and genetic connections of the Gond with the neighbouring populations speaking Indo-European, Dravidian, and Austroasiatic languages. With some separation and differentiation, all Gond groups have a common ancestor. Instead of the other Dravidian tribes to which they are most closely connected linguistically, our allele frequency and haplotype-based analyses show that the Gond share major genetic heritage with the Indian Austroasiatic (i.e. Munda) communities.

Educating the world's largest tribal population is a challenge for India

It cannot be overstated that education is one of the most effective ways to promote socioeconomic development among scheduled tribes.

Initiatives by ministries in the field of tribal education: According to official reports, the Ministry of Tribal Affairs' Education Division, in collaboration with the Ministry of Human Resources Development and the State Governments/UT Administrations, introduced a number of programmes with the aim of expanding access to education in tribal areas by constructing hostels for ST students.

There could be a positive effect from teaching the tribal populations because India has the world's largest population of tribal people. Education is the one significant factor that has the potential to significantly improve the general situation of this tribal group.

An educated youngster is capable of enacting important changes and enhancing the community as a whole.

Furthermore, the entire Indian economy will profit from proper education, not just the tribal population.

Additionally, providing the tribal group with quality educational resources will either immediately improve their situation or ensure that they have better living conditions in the future.

The possible impact of educating the tribal communities:

India has the single largest tribal population in the world. The one major factor that can bring transformation in the overall condition of this tribal population is education.

- An educated youth is capable of collectively bringing in significant changes and improving the whole community

- Moreover, proper education will not just benefit the tribal population but benefit the entire economy of India

- Furthermore, implementing effective education resources for the tribal community will either bring immediate changes in their state of living or improve their future living conditions

The four main language groups and some isolated languages that make up India's linguistic landscape are mostly related to non-overlapping geographic divisions. Indo-European languages, which span a wide geographic area, including northern and western India, are spoken by the majority of the population. With a few exceptions, such as Brahui in Pakistan, Kurukh-Malto in eastern India, and Gondi-Manda languages in central India, Dravidian languages are mostly spoken in southern India. While Tibeto-Burman speakers can be found along the Himalayan edge and in the northeast of the subcontinent, Austroasiatic language speakers are dispersed in pockets, mostly in the eastern and central regions.

In contrast to the caste populations in India, only few tribes exist, with total populations in the millions. The Gond tribe is the most populous and has the most clearly defined clan system of all the central Indian tribes. They number around 12 million people and are primarily situated in eastern central India. There is no exact date for when Gond first appeared on the subcontinent. However, four of their kingdoms are dated to between 1300 and 1600 AD, and they are mentioned in the epic Ramayana. By the Middle Ages, these kingdoms had absorbed so much of the neighbouring Hindu culture's religious and cultural elements that the Gond cultures had developed into a socially more hierarchically structured tribal community.

Gondi, Konda, Kui, Kuvi, Pengo, and Manda are all South Central Dravidian languages that are spoken by various segments of the larger Gond community. The Telugu language, which is mostly spoken in the state of Andhra Pradesh, including Telangana, is the most recent ancestor shared by the Gondi-Manda subgroup in terms of language. According to Robert von Heine-ethnographic Geldern's research, the local ancestral component of the Munda populations and a subset of Dravidian inhabitants represented by the numerous Gond language communities jointly constitute an older layer of the Indian subcontinent's population. Grigson adopted this hypothesis and argued that the Gonds were once a "pre-Dravidian" or "proto-Australoid" population that had undergone significant Dravidian influence. Following his research on the Gond and their closely related Dravidian language communities, Christoph von Fürer-Haimendorf came to the conclusion that these people were the last of an earlier primordial population that had been linguistically absorbed.

There is no other tribe in India's tribal population that can compare to the Gonds in terms of size and historical significance. With a population of well over four million in the late 1970s, the Gonds occupy a sizable portion of the Deccan and play a significant role in the intricate ethnic structure of the region where Indo-Aryan and Dravidian communities coexist.

Concentrations of Gonds remained to live in their traditional way of life in the highlands of the ancient Hyderabad State (now Andhra Pradesh) until the middle of the 20th century: feudal lords continued to act as tribal leaders and hereditary bards retained a treasure of myths and epic tales. Christoph von Fürer-Haimendorf started studying this group of Gonds at that time and spent the better part of three years in their settlements. He saw their everyday activities and intricate ceremonial rituals, and he also recognised the threat that more developed Hindu groups posing as they invaded the Gonds' habitat and vied for their ancestral territory.

Life, Livelihood and Education among the Katkari tribes of Maharashtra

Being one of Maharashtra's most marginalised tribes and having access to few resources, the Katkaris are socially, educationally, and economically underdeveloped. The current study examines the socioeconomic characteristics of the Katkari tribe through an examination of their socioeconomic indicators, including literacy, labour force participation, way of life, occupational pattern, health, and migration. A pilot case study of the Katkari tribes of the 85-hut Godpapad Adivasi Wadi in Maharashtra was carried out to investigate their living situations, means of subsistence, and reasons for having low levels of education. Direct observation and unstructured interviews were utilised as research methodologies to learn more about Katkari people and kids. The investigation indicated poor living circumstances, unstable livelihoods, and minimal education provision in the hamlet, however education was interrupted due to parents' seasonal travel in search of job. India's original inhabitants are the tribal people, who primarily live in the forested areas encircled by hills. They have a distinctive identity that is reflected in their own social structure, culture, language, and territorial affinity. According to its distribution, the tribal zone in India is typically divided into three zones: the north-eastern zone, the central zone, and the southern zone. The Himalayan region, as well as the hill and mountain ranges of North-Eastern India, make up the north-eastern zone. The area to the south of the Krishna River in Peninsular India makes up the southern zone. The central zone is located in the middle of Peninsular India's ancient hills and plateaus that separate it from the Indo Gangetic Plains (Planning Commission, India, 2007). The Katkari tribal community is recognised as the lowest in the social hierarchy by other Scheduled Tribes in the area and is classified as a particularly vulnerable, primitive, and tribal tribe in Maharashtra. Under the Constitution (Scheduled Tribes) order, 1950, the "Katkari" were first acknowledged as a Scheduled Tribe. In Maharashtra, the districts of Raigad, Thane, Pune, Nashik, and Ratnagiri are home to the majority of the Katkaris. (Tomar, 2004). The Katkari tribe is one of Maharashtra's most marginalised, underprivileged, and impoverished. They have restricted access to resources, which contributes to their social, educational, and economic backwardness. In the current study, the researcher conducted a pilot case study to examine the socio-economic indicators of the 85-hut Katkari Adivasi Wadi in Maharashtra, including livelihood, health, occupational pattern, migration, and education. Direct observation and unstructured interviews were utilised as study approaches to learn more about the adults and kids residing in the Godpapad Adivasi Wadi.

Living Conditions in Katkaris

In the Sudhagad Taluka of the Raigad district, around 85 kilometres from Mumbai, Maharashtra, lies the tribal hamlet of Ghorpapad Adiwasi Wadi, which consists of a total of 85 huts or households. At the foothills of the Sahyadri Mountains in Godpapad Adiwasi Wadi, the researcher went to the homes of the Katkari people (Western Ghats). Their huts range in size from 100 to 150 square feet and have thatched roofs and unbaked brick walls that are often kachha or semi-pukka. Cow dung is used to clean the houses' walls and floors. The Katkaris prepare and consume meals using steel utensils and leaf-covered plates, respectively. The furnishings within the house are quite simple and comprise of a few kitchen utensils, a few items of clothing hung from a rope, and equipment for hunting and fishing. The study discovered that the locals use open defecation and lack basic sanitary facilities. They rely on a well for their drinking water, but in times of scarcity, they also use water from open ditches for various household needs, particularly during the monsoon season. Because of the sanitary problems this causes, illnesses including diarrhoea, dysentery, malnutrition, malaria, ringworm, intestinal infections, fever, etc. frequently result. When the researcher questioned some of the tribal members about how they treated illnesses, the Katkari tribal members responded that they only relied on traditional treatments that involved the use of herbal plants, tree roots, and bark, among other things, as well as the traditional knowledge passed down through the generations.

occupations in Katkaris

Due to their predominately landless status, the Katkaris' traditional means of subsistence include hunting with crude tools and gathering insignificant forest products. They were compelled to relocate to the foothills of the forests, depriving them of their principal source of livelihood, as a result of government measures to stop deforestation and combat resource depletion. After speaking with a few Katkari males, the researcher learned that they are currently primarily engaged in two separate jobs, not simultaneously but rather in a cyclic fashion. They claimed to be agricultural labourers for other landed tribal ethnic groups in the neighbourhood from June to November, with the male members working as farm servants (known as gadi in the local language) and the womenfolk as daily paid labourers. These fields are primarily used for the production of rice, with ragi, udid (pulses), and khurasni (a regional kind of oilseed) serving as auxiliary crops. However, they claimed that because agriculture in these farmlands is dependent on rainfall and there are no options for irrigation, there is no room for double-cropping and as a result, these Katkari tribal people are left jobless at the conclusion of each agricultural season. To ensure their financial and food security, the Katkari men travel to other areas between December and May in search of work (mainly to other parts of Maharashtra, Andhra Pradesh, and Karnataka). They work in brick kilns. In order to support themselves and their families, the majority of Katkari males (about 98 percent) from Godpapad Adiwasi hamlet migrate to different regions of the nation during this periodic movement.

The Katkari are one of the only tribal communities in India that consumes rodents like the Indian bandicoot, black rat, and little Indian field mouse. They think that consuming rodent meat gives them strength and a long life.

Even though it was shown that 69.5 percent of Katkari youngsters had had any vaccinations, there was a substantial dropout rate for each shot.

The Eco-friendly Tharu Tribe

The Tharu culture is particularly environmentally conscious; all of this tribe's customs and practises have a strong connection to the natural world. They depend on nature for their homes, food, clothing, clothes, art, religion, economy, and many other aspects of life in order to maintain ecological equilibrium. The Earth, known to the Tharu as "Bhumsen" in their native tongue, is the principal deity they worship. In this society, the family structure is strong. In their family system, women enjoy high standing and sufficient social and economic rights. Although there is a patriarchal family system in this town, women have higher status and more rights, which is a measurable truth. Youth in Tharu prefer to change, thus they are competing for advancement. The process of cultural exchange is ongoing in the Tharu area because there are several other groups there thanks to industrialization and business. Tharu adolescents are drawn to a novel and alluring way of life. The old Tharu culture is under peril because they are ignoring their original tribal customs. They must receive modern education, communication, and technological advancements, etc. To maintain their identity, however, traditional culture must also be preserved.

The great Andamanese

The Andamanese, at least those who live on the southern island, don't build any form of dwelling. They enjoy sandy beaches with towering cliffs that provide wind protection. I frequently stumble across one of their makeshift homes when strolling down the beach close to Port Mouat; it consists of a hole dug out in the sand beneath an overhanging rock that can fit a single person. They rarely spend consecutive nights in the same sleeping arrangements. The people of the tiny Andaman build gigantic cottages that resemble beehives, with roofs that are almost at ground level. Their creation of strange objects like moving fish spears and arrows shows great innovation and the use of strong thinking to match means to ends. The arrow head, which is manufactured from iron taken from ships that have sunk nearby, is a triangular piece of flattened iron that is attached to the end of a short stick that is about four inches long. One to three iron barbs are also attached to the stick at the base of the head. This short stick's tip fits into a socket that is made for it at the very end of the arrow's shaft. A flattened thong (made of wood fibres) about eight inches long, linked at one end to the distal end of the shaft and at the other to the stick holding the head, also serves to preserve the connection between the head and shaft. They most likely learned how to build them through watching the Nicobarese huts on the nearby island of Car-Nicobar during some of their expeditions or by receiving instruction from their Nicobarese prisoners.

CHAPTER THREE

IMPACT OF BARSA MUNDA ON INDIAN TRIBAL COMMUNITIES AND HIS MESSAGE TO HUMANITY

Introduction

Not only did Birsa Munda battle the British, but he also supported the interests of tribal people and helped to dismantle the feudal system in Jharkhand and Bihar that ravaged the Adivasi lands. In the Chhotanagpur Plateau region, Birsa Munda was an Indian tribal freedom fighter, religious leader and folk hero belonging to the Munda tribe.

When we think about the Indian fight for independence, a list about names springs to mind immediately. But for every Mahatma Gandhi, Jawaharlal Nehru, Lokmanya Tilak or Bhagat Singh, history has forgotten thousands of heroes. And also, in our history textbooks, there are others who helped start the war long previous to the dates. Birsa Munda was one such pioneering freedom fighter. In the Chhotanagpur Plateau region, Birsa Munda was an Indian tribal freedom fighter, religious leader and folk hero belonging to the Munda tribe. In the 19th century, under the Bengal Presidency, Birsa Munda began a tribal nationalist Millennial Campaign. On November 15, Birsa Munda was born,Birsa Munda was born in Ulihatu, Bengal's Presidency (present-day Jharkhand), on November 15, 1875, to Sugana Munda and Karmi Hatu.

Munda went to a missionary school, where Jaipal Nag, his tutor, persuaded his sharp young student to resume his studies and enrol in the German Mission School. He was forced to convert to Christianity because of this.

Munda spent a great deal of time between 1886 and 1890 in Chaibasa, Jharkhand, which was similar to the agitation of the Sardars against the British government. Munda wanted to renounce Christianity and abandon the German Mission School, profoundly affected and disillusioned by what he saw the British and Christian missionaries doing to the Indians there.

As a prophet, Birsa Munda

Birsa learnt about Hindu religious doctrines from a Vaishnav monk and, along with the Ramayana and Mahabharata, read the ancient scriptures. He wore the holy string, worshipped the plant of tulsi, and gave up the meat.

He encouraged them to let go of practises in witchcraft and, instead, emphasised the importance of fasting, keeping away from drinking, having faith in God and following a code of behaviour. Birsa decided to change the tribal community.

'Father of the Earth'

He went on to establish a new faith called Birsait, where only one deity was worshipped. Birsait soon became the common religion among the Mundas and Oraons, considering his increasing presence in the tribal culture. Munda, nicknamed 'Dharti Abba' or Father of the World, urged his disciples to return and adopt their customs to their tribal origins.

Munda also preached a potent anti-British sentiment through his faith and recruited thousands of tribal folk to form guerrilla forces to attack the Raj. In the late 1890s, Munda set out to dismantle the feudal system imposed by the British in the forest territory of the Adivasi. The British welcomed settlers from other states to come and take over jobs on tribal land in this scheme, although they pocketed all the earnings. The separate tribes, who were the original owners of the land, were thus left stripped of property and any means of subsistence. In the states of Odisha, Bihar , West Bengal and Madhya Pradesh, his slogan targeting the British Raj is still remembered today. The slogan was "Abua raj seter jana, maharani raj tundu jana," meaning "Let the queen's kingdom end and our kingdom be created."

Birsa asked his fellow tribesman in 1895 to renounce Christianity and led them to worship one God and to show them the direction of purity, abstinence and forbidden cow-slaughters Furthermore, he claimed to be a prophet and said that Queen Victoria 's reign was over and the Munda Raj had begun. His followers declared that their real enemies were the British and not the Christian Mundas.

Birsa Munda and his succession

The legacy of Birsa Munda is still alive, and on November 15, the tribal people of Karnataka and Jharkhand commemorate their birth anniversary. Several colleges and organisations are named after him — Birsa Agricultural University, Birsa Technology Institute, Birsa Khunti College, Birsa Sindri Technology Institute, Sidho Kanho Birsha University, Birsa Munda Athletics Stadium, Birsa Munda Airport, Birsa Munda Central Prison, Birsa Seva Dal, Birsa Munda Tribal University.

Birsa, a pioneer and brave warrior of fredom, saw the injustice put on his felllow tribals. He gathered them in a party and led agitation against the forceful seizure by non-tribals and then country-British rulers of the land of tribals.

The aim of his movement was to prevent his fellow tribals from becoming bonded labourers and to check their wealth's exploitation. Birsa urged the tribals to stick to their rich culture and traditions, urging them not to step under any pressure.

His birthday, which falls on 15 November, is also celebrated by tribal people in the districts of Mysore and Kodagu in Karnataka, and official functions take place in his Samadhi Sthal, in the capital of Jharkhand, Kokar Ranchi.

He died at the very early age of 25, but the foundations of British society were broken by his deeds and agitations. Birsa began the 'Ulgulan' or 'The Great Tumult' movement. His battle against tribal deprivation and prejudice culminated in a significant hit in 1908 against the British government in the form of the Chotanagpur Tenancy Act. The act limited the transferring of land to non-tribals from the tribal people. His campaign compelled the Colonial government to pass the Tenancy Act of Chhotanagpur, 1908. The product of his committed fight against the injustice faced by the tribals was this act.

On 3 March 1900, when he was sleeping alongside his tribal rebel army battling British troops, he was arrested in Jamkopai forest, Chakradharpur. Around 460 tribal persons were convicted, one of whom was given capital punishment, 39 were awarded lifetime transportation, and 23 were sentenced to 14 years in prison. Birsa Munda died of cholera in Ranchi gaol on 9 June 1900.

Birsa Munda began to spread the Hindu religion's values and urged converting tribal people to fully read their original belief structure. He is such a notable figure that his blessings were claimed by tribal citizens.

Birsa Munda believed in modern education and speaking out against societal ills: PM

On November 13, on the first-ever "Janjatiya Gaurav Divas," or day celebrating tribal pride, Prime Minister Narendra Modi made an effort to reach out to tribal people. He opened the Birsa Munda museum in Ranchi and a number of social programmes in Bhopal. On November 13, 2021, at Jamboree Ground in Bhopal, Mr. Modi addressed the event, saying, "After Independence, for the first time in the country, on such a large scale, the art-culture of the entire country's tribal society, their contribution to the freedom movement and nation-building is being remembered and honoured with pride."

On what was the first-ever "Janjatiya Gaurav," Prime Minister Narendra Modi on Monday showed his support for tribal people by opening the Birsa Munda museum in Ranchi and a number of charity programmes in Bhopal.

On Monday, the first-ever "Janjatiya Gaurav Divas," or day celebrating tribal pride, Prime Minister Narendra Modi made an effort to reach out to tribal people. He opened the Birsa Munda museum in Ranchi and a number of charity programmes in Bhopal. In Ranchi earlier that day, he opened the first of ten new museums honouring tribal culture and its contributions to the freedom movement as well as the anniversary of the birth of tribal freedom hero Birsa Munda.

On the first "Janjatiya Gaurav Diwas," or day of tribal pride, Mr. Modi opened the Bhagwan Birsa Munda memorial and freedom fighter museum.

Speaking virtually to the group, he said that in honour of the nation's upcoming 75th anniversary of independence, tribal people will be recognised for their accomplishments.For this reason, a historic decision has been made, according to which the nation will now annually commemorate November 15 as "Janjatiya Gaurav Diwas," or the anniversary of Bhagwan Birsa Munda's birth. In his remarks at the Bhopal event, Prime Minister Modi said, "After Independence, for the first time in the country, on such a large scale, the art-culture of the entire country's tribal society, their contribution to the freedom movement and nation-building is being remembered and honoured with pride."

When the role of tribal society in nation-building was described, some people were taken aback because the country had not been informed of these details. He claimed that "this happened because people who ruled the country for decades following Independence paid primacy to their own political agendas."

ANALYSIS AND DISCUSSION

- Munda still emphasised the need for tribals to recognise their privileges, history and tackle the oppression they are facing. He was also trying to rationalise his culture and get rid of their superstitious practises, sacrificing of cattle, and alcohol.
- The tribal leader, who was also a key force in the fight for a separate statehood for Jharkhand, spearheaded the movement to abolish the feudal system in Jharkhand and Bihar that plagued the Adivasi lands.
- He assembled tribal people in October 1894 and marched for the remission of taxes received from the tribes by the Zamindars. The British began shooting on the local tribal population to stop this campaign, and hundreds of tribal people lost their lives.
- Birsa was detained by the British a few months after the campaign. On June 9, 1900, at the age of 25, in Ranhi Jail, he took his last breath. The British authorities believed that he died of cholera even though he had no signs of the disease. Several tribal leaders suggested that he may have been killed by the prison authorities. The British, however, enforced the Chota Nagpur Tenancy Act eight years after his death, which prohibited the selling of Adivasi land to non-Adivasis.
- In literature and mass media, the young revolutionist continues to be praised for his impressive and courageous campaign against the British to grant native land rights.

CONCLUSION

To the missionaries, Birsa 's assertion to be a prophet of God and the creation of a new faith seemed ridiculous. Birsa Munda began to urge tribal people to follow their original conventional religious tribal system.[10] He became a prophet figure to the tribal people, impressed by his teachings, and they sought his blessings. In a series of revolts and uprisings under his rule, Birsa and the Munda reacted to the twin threats of agrarian breakdown and cultural transition. In 1895, Birsa Munda renounced Christianity in Chalakkad village of Tamar, invited his fellow tribesmen to worship only one Deity and leave the worship of bongas. It is proposed to build in Jharkhand a 150-foot-tall statue of Ulgulan (Birsa Munda). The stones that are to be used in the monument are obtained from the area's nearby houses. In the Indian Parliament Museum, his portrait hangs; he is the only tribal chief to have been so honoured.

In areas of Odisha, Bihar , West Bengal, and Madhya Pradesh, Birsa Munda's slogan threatening the British Raj-Abua raj seter jana, maharani raj tundu jana ("Let the queen's kingdom be ended and our kingdom be established") is remembered today. The campaign diminished after his death. The Chotanagpur Tenancy Act (CNT), which forbids the sale of tribal land to non-tribals, was implemented by the colonial government in 1908. This courageous and robust man died fighting for the country and his tribe. The nation will never forget what he did for the Indians.

His courage not only helped his tribe, but also instilled in the people of the whole country the emotions of nationalism. Birsa Munda was not able to live to see the flame that had begun to turn into a fire.

CHAPTER FOUR

THE CHALLANGES AND OPPORTUNITIES OF TRIBAL EDUCATION IN INDIA

Introduction

Education is one of the essential requirements for man-making and nation building. It is indispensible for development of human resources. Education imparts knowledge, skills, and character. After independence, the governments in India relied more on literacy mission emphasizing 3Rs (Reading, Writing and Arithmetic) to fulfill the expectations of the Directive Principles of State Policy. At the backdrop of the New Education Policy, likely to come up shortly, the paper makes a critical attempt to appraise the statistics and status of the education among Tribes across India. The objective of this paper is to identify the problems of Tribal Education in India and to find out solutions. The present paper reveals that the tribal people are still lagging behind in all stages of education and they are facing various problems in education. It further mentions some suggestions for improvement of tribal education in India.

Education for all (EFA) is an international commitment to ensure that every child receives basic education of good quality. But education for all has not been given sufficient attention to some marginalized groups of children in some of the developing countries like India. Our constitution laid down numerous provisions for uplift of tribal communities but still they are confronted with various challenges. Despite several initiatives taken by the Government to enhance educational status ever since independence, the literacy rate among Schedule Tribes has remained low. Scheduled Tribes are geographically, socially isolated and economically marginalized communities. In the post-Independence period, sincere and concerted efforts were made for the economic and educational development of tribal's. Despite these efforts the performance of the tribes in education is much lower than the Scheduled Castes. As the studies on tribal education suggests that the policy makers approach paid little attention to culturally linked education. This has led to drop outs and directly impacted their overall educational status.

India is a home to a large variety of indigenous people. The Scheduled Tribe population represents one of the most economically impoverished and marginalized groups in India. With a population of more than 10.2crores, India has the single largest tribal population in the world. This constitutes 8.6 per cent of the total population of the country (Census of India, 2011). Sahu (2014) stated that "there are over 500 tribes (with many overlapping communities in more than one State) as notified under article 342 of the Constitution of India, spread over different States and Union Territories of the country" (p. 1). The tribal groups are found in hilly areas and rely upon the environmental situations for the sustenance of their living conditions. In tribal groups the system of education is not in a well-developed state. Despite consistent efforts each with the aid of Central and State governments to unfold the schooling of scheduled tribes and other weaker sections, the extent of schooling amongst scheduled Tribes could be very low in comparison to general population (Andrabi & Jabeen, 2018). For promoting effective growth and improvement of the country, it is far necessary to place emphasis upon the impartment of primary literacy competencies amongst tribal students.

India is shifting in the direction of inclusive growth however loss of education, skills development and transparent governance are a few hurdles in progressing toward it at a quicker tempo (Sahu, 2014). Regardless of constitutional provisions and safe guard with different government activities and programme, educating tribal child is as yet a significant worry for the public authority. Daripa (2017) mentioned in his research work that "there are so many socio-cultural, economical, geographical, and administrative obstacle (report Ministry of Tribal Affairs, GOI, 2013) for which literacy rate of tribal people has never been at par with entire population, and gap between them is always high, for example the gap between tribals and whole population in literacy rate was 19.7% in 1961 which increased to 21.6% in 1991 and has declined to 14.3% in 2011" (p. 163). A country's improvement is straightforwardly identified with the availability and opportunities to avail educational facilities by the people. It is a generally acknowledged idea that education serves as a pivot for the tribals to build up a kinship with the remainder of the Indian populace.

Education, especially in its elementary form, is considered of utmost importance to the tribals because it's crucial for total development of tribal communities and is particularly helpful to build confidence among the tribes to deal with outsiders on equal terms. Despite the sincere and concerted efforts by the government for the overall development of the scheduled tribes, they are still far behind in almost all the standard parameters of development. They are not able to participate in the process of development, as they are not aware of most of the progrmmes and policies made for their upliftment. This is mainly due to the high incidence of illiteracy and very low level of education among the tribal people. Hence, the educational status of the scheduled tribes and the role of governance in this direction are highly essential. It is well known that the educational background of tribes is very discouraging as compared to the rest of the population. So, education is an important avenue for upgrading the economic and social conditions of the Scheduled Tribes. In this context, the objective of this paper is to analyse the trend of literacy rate, gross enrolment ratio, dropout rates and Gender Parity Index of tribal education in India.

Development should not be studied in isolation. Development is not synonymous with the growth of a few affluent persons. As Amartya Sen (1999) stated unless the capabilities among human beings are adequately addressed and deprivations faced by marginalized groups are overcome, development cannot take place. In fact he stressed on the capabilities and human freedoms, and this freedom can only be achieved when the people are guaranteed political freedom, economic facilities, social opportunities, transparency, and security. Although these conditions are different from one another, they are all inter-connected.

Constitutional safeguard for Tribal Education

In post independence India sparkling initiatives have been taken for tribal development by changing the sooner coverage of indifference. The Government of India recommended a policy, which could combine the welfare and socioeconomic elevation of the tribes. With the adoption of the constitution, the promoting of education of tribes has grown to be a unique duty of the Governments. The framers of our Constitution have given certain special facilities and securities to the tribes. These facilities and securities offer some shielding discrimination to the tribes against the non-tribes. The advent of scheduled areas for tribe's overall performance in admissions to instructional institutions and public offerings and the supply of incentives for schooling are a number of mechanisms visualized to meet the constitutional guidelines (Akula, 2013).

Article 45 of the Constitution is more specific regarding obligation of the state. It directs the state to strive to provide with a period of 10 years from the commencement of the constitution free and compulsory education up to the age of 14 years. Article 46 of the Constitution directs to promote with special care the education and economic interest of the weaker sections of the society and in particular scheduled caste and scheduled tribes. Beside the Constitutional provisions, the main bases of educational policy in India are several commissions and committees appointed from time to time to suggest reforms in the educational system so as to meet adequately the emerging educational needs and demands of the country. Article 154(4) empowers the state to make any special provision for the advancement of any socially and educationally backward classes of citizen or for SCs or STs. Article 29(1) provides distinct languages script or culture. This article has special significance for scheduled tribes. Untouchability is abolished under Article 17, and its practice in any form is a punishable offence Article 275(1) provides Grants in-Aids to states (having scheduled tribes) covered under fifth and six schedules of the constitution. Article 350A states that "It shall be the endeavor of every state and every local authority within the state to provide adequate facilities for instruction in mother-tongue at the primary stage of education to the children belonging to the minority group". Article 243D, 330, and article 332 provides reservation of seats for STs in gram panchayat, house of people and state legislative assembly. The Right to Education Act, which was implemented in 2009, stated that all children, belonging to the age group of six to fourteen years have the right to free and compulsory education.

Though, number of initiations has been taken for the development of schooling amongst tribal communities no great development has taken region due to an intergenerational vicious cycle of poverty, illiteracy and deprivation. This is evident in extraordinarily negative grownup literacy rates that are reproduced as low schooling ranges amongst children from tribal groups. Education, in its broadest sense, refers to the approaches in which people analyze competencies and advantage knowledge and understanding about the world, and approximately themselves. Most countries spend a massive amount of time and money to provide schooling for their residents. But that is lacking within the tribal belt which creates new problems (Akula, 2013).

Rationale of the study

India has a rich glorious heritage, but a sizeable part of Indian population is yet to get benefits out of it. They are still tribal communities which are primitive and live in secluded areas (Verma 1996). The Imperial Gazetteer of India, 1911 defines tribe as a "collection of families bearing a common name, speaking a common dialect, occupying or professing to occupy a common territory and is not usually endogamous though originally it might have been so" (Nithya 2014). According to D.N. Majumdar "A tribe is a social group with territorial afflation, endogamous with no specialization of functions, rule by tribal officers, hereditary or otherwise united in language and dialect, recognizing social distance with other tribes or caste without any social obloquy attaching to them, as it does in the caste structure, following tribal traditions, beliefs and customs, illiberal of naturalization of ideas, from alien sources, above all conscious of homogeneity of ethnic and territorial integration" (quoted in Varma 1996). The tribes in India usually reside in hill areas, forests, near the seas, and in islands. Their life style is quite different from non-tribals (Preet 1994). It is not that their societies are static, but the pace of social change in tribal society is very slow. Since they are materially and economically backward, attempts have been made by the Government to develop them. Today, the governments in all countries are paying special attention to development of the tribes (Nithya 2014). Though our national leaders and constitutional makers are committed to uplift the tribal people, a desired level of development has not been achieved yet (Chandra Guru et. al: 2015).

Problems of Tribal Education

There are many critical issues and problems in the field of tribal education. They are as follows:

- **Medium of language**: Language is one of the important constraints of tribal children which prevents them access to education. English or regional languages are used as the medium of teaching in the schools. The tribal people have their own separate dialect so that their children couldn't understand whatever taught in the class rooms. This phenomena lowers the educational level of tribal children. Language and culture are regarded as significant barriers that tribal students experience within the course of acquisition of education. They have their own cultures, traditions, norms, values and principles, upon which their livelihood opportunities are based. Furthermore, they also speak different languages. Research has indicated that due to differences in language, they experience problems in establishing effective communication terms with teachers as well as fellow students. These differences also become major impediments within the course of understanding academic concepts and achievement of goals and objectives.

- **The Location of the Village:**The physical barrier creates a hindrance for the children of a tribal village to attend the school in a neighboring village.

- **Economic Condition:** The economic condition of tribal people is so poor that they do not desire to spare their children or their labour power and allow them to attend schools. Finances are regarded to be of utmost significance within the course of implementation of various tasks and activities. Within the course of acquisition of education, financial problems are regarded as major barriers. The tribal communities are regarded as poverty stricken and most exploited (Mukherjee, 2009). The tribal individuals are usually residing in the conditions of poverty and backwardness. Agriculture, hunting and fishing are their primary occupations. Income generated in used to sustain their living conditions. Therefore, due to financial problems, the parents encourage their children to get engaged in income-generating activities. In this manner, as a result of financial problems, the tribal students experience challenges within the course of acquisition of education (Kapur, 2019). The tribal communities normally are residing in the conditions of poverty and backwardness. They have the major objective of generating income for sustaining their living conditions in an appropriate manner. The primary income-generating activities that tribal communities are engaged in are, agriculture and farming practices and production of food items, handicrafts, artworks and so forth. The individuals usually encourage their children to participate in income-generating activities. Hence, when children are required to assist their parents in income-generating activities, they experience challenges within the course of acquisition of education.

- **Attitude of the parents:** As education does not yield any immediate economic return, the tribal parents prefer to engage their children in remunerative employment which supplements the family income. Within the course of academic learning, students need support and assistance from not only individuals within schools, such as, teachers and fellow students, but also parents. In tribal communities, the support of parents is negligible. The tribal children are unable to acquire support from their parents in the implementation of academic assignments. This is regarded as one of the major challenges within the course of acquisition of education. Tribal parents are basically illiterate. Their illiteracy does not permit them to understand the long term values of education. As education does not yield them any immediate economic return, they prefer to engage their children in remunerative employment which supplements the family income and strengthens the family economy. Further a few parents who have become aware of the values of education, fail to accord education to their children as they cannot afford finances for it.

- **Teacher Related Problems:**In the remote tribal areas the teacher absenteeism is a regular phenomenon and this affects largely the quality of education. In tribal villages, villagers have virtually no relationship with the teachers. Teachers do not get any accommodation facility in the village, which makes them irregular which hampers the normal routine of a school. Further, the apathetic attitude of the villagers and the appointment of untrained teachers in tribal areas diminish the values of education. In schools in tribal communities, the teaching-learning methods are either not adequately available or the ones that are utilized are not in accordance to the academic requirements of students. It is apparent that when adequate teaching-learning methods would not be put into practice, then certainly students will experience problems within the course of acquisition of academic concepts. The major factors that lead to unsatisfactory teaching-learning methods are, the curriculum content is inappropriate and medium of instruction takes place in language, which is not known to the tribal children. Learning materials are regarded to be of utmost significance to acquire understanding of academic concepts and achieve academic goals. They are the ones that impart knowledge and information among students regarding various aspects and concepts. These include textbooks, technologies, internet, diagrams, charts, models, posters and other reading materials. The tribal students experience lack of learning materials. Due to their conditions of poverty and lack of financial resources, they are unable to obtain sufficient learning materials.

- **Lack of Proper monitoring:**Proper monitoring is hindered by poor coordination between the Tribal Welfare Department and School Education Department.
- **Management of Household Responsibilities:** In tribal communities, the children are usually involved in the management of household responsibilities. They assist their parents in various household chores like fetching water, cleaning, washing, preparation of meals, agricultural activities and collection of forest products, rearing of livestock and looking after younger siblings. Therefore, when children are encouraged to participate in management of household responsibilities, they are unable to attend schools.
- **Low Levels of Motivation:** It is essential for students to possess interest, enthusiasm and high levels of motivation, particularly within the course of attainment of academic goals. Tribal students usually possess low levels of motivation. The primary causes are, lack of efficient understanding of academic concepts, learning disabilities, unavailability of learning materials, lack of infrastructure and other facilities and lack of support from parents, particularly in academic learning. As a consequence, the students either experience low academic performance or drop out from schools, before their educational skills are honed.
- **Lack of Facilities and Amenities:** In tribal schools, there are lack of facilities and amenities. The major facilities that are necessary to enhance the system of education are, appropriate teaching-learning materials, technologies, furniture, heating and cooling equipment in accordance to the weather conditions, clean drinking water, restrooms, library facilities, laboratory facilities, playgrounds, extra-curricular and creative activities and other materials that are essential to carry out the job duties in an appropriate manner. These facilities and amenities are not in a well-developed state in tribal schools. Hence, this has proved to be a major challenge within the course of acquisition of education.
- **Health Problems:** As it has been stated that tribal communities depend upon the natural environmental conditions for their survival. In case of any health problems, or illnesses, they obtain medicinal herbs and plants from the forests. The tribal communities adopt traditional methods and are unaware of modern and advanced medical and health care treatment. In their environmental conditions, they do not have access to medical or health care centres. Health problems experienced by tribal children

are regarded as major impediments within the course of acquisition of education.

- **External Problems:** The perspective adopted for educational development among tribal communities fails to adequately address the specific disadvantages characterizing tribal population. For instance, the population and distance norms formed by the government have not been beneficial to tribal locations because of their sparse population and sporadic residential patterns. Further, in formulating policies and programmes for tribal education it is essential to understand the complex realities of tribal life and the expectation of tribals from the system, and this has never been done either by the tribal welfare department or by the education department. Consequently, no worthwhile policy for tribal education has been formed.

- **Internal Problems:** The internal problems of tribal education refer to the quality of school provision, suitable teachers, relevance of content and curriculum, medium of instruction, pedagogy, and special supervision. A majority of schools in tribal areas are without basic infrastructure facilities. Normally, school buildings in tribal areas have thatched roofs, dilapidated walls, and non-plastered floors. Schools in tribal areas just function with bare minimum facilities.

Government Policies and Programmes for Tribal Education:

Starting from the First Five Year Plan Period1 (1951-1956) the government is steadily allocating financial resources for the purpose of tribal development. Towards, the end of the plan (1954), 43 Special Multipurpose Tribal Development Projects (MTDPs) were created. During the Third Five Year Plan Period (1961-1966), the government of India adopted the strategy of converting areas with more than 66 per cent tribal concentration into Tribal Development Blocks (TBDs). By the end of Fourth Five Year Plan (1969-1974), the number of TBDs in the country rose to 504. Additionally, in 1972 the Tribal Sub-Plan Strategy (TSP) was implemented by the Ministry of Education and Social Welfare. TSP was based on twin objectives of socio-economic development and protection against exploitation. It was generally implemented in the areas where the Scheduled Tribe population was more than 50 per cent of the total population.

The PESA (The Panchayats Extension to Scheduled Areas) Act, 1996 in fact, has made it mandatory for the States having scheduled areas to make specific provisions for giving wide-ranging powers to the tribes on the matters relating to decision-making and development of their community. A centrally-sponsored government scheme of ashram schools exclusively for ST children from elementary to higher secondary levels was initiated in the 1970s. But the poor quality of education in ashram schools, however, has undermined confidence in education as a vehicle for social mobility.

The Janshala Programme is a collaborative effort of the Government of India (GOI) and five UN Agencies –UNDP, UNICEF, UNESCO, ILO and UNFPA –a community based primary education programme, aims to make primary education more accessible and effective, especially for girls and children in deprived communities, marginalised groups, Scheduled Caste/ Scheduled Tribes/minorities, children with specific needs.

Suggestions: Some suggestions for improvement of tribal education are as follows-

- **Literacy Campaign:** Proper awareness campaign should be organized to create the awareness about the importance of education. Extensive literacy campaign in the tribal dominated districts may be undertaken on a priority basis to literate the tribal.
- **Attitude of the Tribal parents:**The attitude of the tribal parents toward education should be improved through proper counseling and guidance.
- **Relevant Study Materials in local languages:** All study materials should be supplied in local languages of tribes.
- **Appointment of Local teachers and Female teachers:** It is suggested to appoint more tribal teachers and female teachers in the tribal areas. The ecological, cultural, psychological characteristics of tribal children should be considered carefully by the teachers in tribal areas.
- **Stipends and Various Scholarships:** Since higher education among the tribes is less, special ST Scholarships should be provided to the tribal students perusing higher education, particularly in medical, engineering, and other vocational streams.
- **Residential Schools:**More residential schools should be established in each states and districts and extended up to PG level in tribal areas.
- **Social Security:**Social security of students, especially of adolescent girls is of great concern in residential schools.
- **Proper Monitoring:**Higher level officials should check the functioning of schools frequently relating to the teaching methods, working hours, and attendance registers.

- Government should take some specific initiative through various programmes like awareness camp, street drama, counseling, etc which can create awareness among the tribals about the importance of education.
- Teachers should be locally recruited who understand and respect tribal culture and practices and most importantly are acquainted with the local language.
- Infrastructural requirement has always been neglected. It should be taken under consideration. School in tribal areas should be furnished with adequate class rooms, teaching aids, electricity, water supply, separate toilet for girls and boys, boundary walls, play ground etc.
- New teacher training institutes should be opened in tribal sub plan areas to meet the requirement of trained teachers. Teaching and learning should be imparted in local language. Emphasis should be given to career or job oriented courses.
- There are no sufficient higher secondary schools in tribal areas, so government needs to establish residential school in such areas under various governmental schemes.
- There must be strong machinery to protect students from abuse, neglect, exploitation, and violence.
- Proper awareness campaign should be organized to create the awareness about the importance of education. Extensive literacy campaign in the tribal dominated districts may be undertaken on a priority basis to literate the tribal.
- The attitude of the tribal parents toward education should be improved through proper counseling and guidance. All study materials should be supplied in local languages of tribes.
- Since higher education among the tribes is less, special ST scholarships should be provided to the tribal students perusing higher education, particularly in medical, engineering, and other vocational streams.
- Higher level officials should check the functioning of schools frequently relating to the teaching methods, working hours, and attendance registers.
- Teachers must be sensitized to the cultural and behavioral strengths of tribal children and motivated to do their best for them in schools. Incentives should be initiated to attract effective teachers to work in tribal schools and to retain them there. Only such motivated teachers are likely to generate interest among tribal children towards schools

education.

- To improve attendance of the tribal students, more number of residential ashram schools is opened in the tribal areas.

Conclusion

Education is the key to tribal development. Education is a crucial road for upgrading the monetary and social situations of the Scheduled Tribes. Tribal children have very low levels of participation and achievement in school education programmes. A clean coverage for local language use in schools is vital for inclusive growth. Though the improvement of the tribes is taking area in India, but the tempo of improvement has been instead gradual. If government will no longer take a few drastic steps for the improvement of tribal education, the status of education amongst tribes could be a story of misery, melancholy and death. Hence time has come to suppose it critically approximately tribal education and inclusive growth. So, there is a pressing need for numerous government interventions, planners and policy makers to cope with this problem and allocate more funds in the central and state budgets for tribal education. Easy access and more opportunities have to be furnished to the tribal children in order to bring them to the mainstream of financial development. The tribal people are very sensitive, their problems are in some recognize complex. Tribal own form of tradition and way of life associated with nature that's the want of the hour to keep and hold for beneficial use in destiny inside the human society. Though the development of the tribes is taking place in India, but the pace of development has been rather slow. If govt. will not take some drastic steps for the development of tribal education, the status of education among tribes will be a story of distress, despair and death. Hence time has come to think it seriously about tribal education and inclusive growth. So, there is an urgent need for various govt. interventions, planners and policy makers to address this problem and allocate more funds in the central and state budgets for tribal education. Easy access and more opportunities should be provided to the tribal children in order to bring them to the mainstream of economic development.

CHAPTER FIVE

PROBLEMS OF TRIBAL EDUCATION IN INDIA

Introduction:

Native Indians come from a wide range of ethnicities. One of India's most economically disadvantaged and disenfranchised groups is the Scheduled Tribe people. India is the country with the biggest concentration of tribal people in the world, with a total population of over 10.2 billion. 8.6% of the nation's overall population is represented by this. According to May academics, there are over 500 tribes distributed across the nation's States and Union Territories (many of which have overlapping communities in more than one State), as notified by article 342 of the Indian Constitution. The environment is what sustains the living conditions of the tribal communities, which are situated in hilly places. The educational system is not well-developed in tribal groups. Despite ongoing efforts made with the help of the federal and state governments to improve education for scheduled tribes and other underprivileged groups, scheduled tribes may have very low levels of schooling compared to the general population. Accentuating the teaching of basic reading skills to tribal students is crucial for fostering the effective growth and improvement of the nation.

India is moving toward inclusive growth, but several obstacles are preventing it from happening more quickly. These include the loss of education, the lack of skill development, and transparent governance. Even with constitutional safeguards and other government initiatives and programs, teaching an indigenous child remains a top concern for the public authority. The ease with which people can access and take advantage of educational opportunities reveals a nation's development. Education, it is widely believed, acts as a turning point for tribal members to develop ties with the rest of the Indian population.

Tribal education is protected under the constitution:

India has made brilliant post-independence efforts to promote tribal development by reversing the earlier trend of neglect. The Indian government suggested a course of action that would combine the welfare and socioeconomic advancement of the tribes. The promotion of tribal education has become a special responsibility of the governments since the passage of the constitution. The people who drafted our Constitution have granted the tribes a few specific privileges and security measures. These amenities and security measures provide some protection from prejudice on the part of tribes against non-tribes. Several measures were envisioned to comply with the constitutional requirements, including the introduction of scheduled areas for the tribe's overall performance in admissions to educational institutions and public offers as well as the provision of educational incentives.

The obligation of the state is more specifically outlined in Article 45 of the Constitution. It commands the government to make every effort to offer 10 years from the constitution's inception of free and obligatory education for children up to the age of 14.

The weaker segments of society, particularly those belonging to scheduled castes and scheduled tribes, are to have their economic and educational interests promoted with special consideration, according to Article 46 of the Constitution. In addition to the provisions of the Constitution, the main pillars of Indian educational policy are several commissions and committees that are periodically appointed to make recommendations for changes to the educational system to adequately address the nation's changing educational needs and demands.

The state is given the authority to adopt any special provisions under Article 154(4) for the advancement of SCs or STs or any other socially or educationally disadvantaged classes of citizens.

According to Article 29(1), different languages, scripts, or cultures exist. For scheduled tribes, this topic has special significance.

Under Article 17, untouchability is outlawed, and engaging in it in any way is a crime. States with scheduled tribes covered by the fifth and sixth schedules of the constitution are eligible for grants of aid under Article 275(1).

According to Article 350A, "any State shall attempt to offer suitable facilities for instruction in the mother tongue at the elementary stage of education to the children belonging to the Minority Group."

Seats are reserved for STs in the gram panchayat, house of people, and state legislative assembly under Articles 243D, 330, and 332.

According to the Right to Education Act, which went into effect in 2009, all children between the ages of six and fourteen have the legal right to a free, public education.

Due to an intergenerational cycle of poverty, illiteracy, and deprivation, despite several endeavors for the establishment of schools among indigenous people, little progress has been made. Extremely low adult literacy rates, which are replicated as low schooling levels among children from tribal cultures, are evidence of this. In its broadest definition, education refers to the methods through which individuals assess their skills and gain information and awareness about the outside world as well as themselves. The majority of nations invest a significant amount of time and money in educating their citizens. However, the tribal belt lacks that, which brings forth fresh issues.

The challenge faced by tribal students in obtaining an education:

The following have been listed as the main issues that tribal students face when pursuing an education:

I) **Financial Issues:** When carrying out various chores and activities, finances are seen as being of the utmost importance. Financial issues are seen as one of the biggest obstacles to obtaining an education. The poorest and most exploited societies are generally considered to be tribal tribes. Typically, tribal members live in impoverished, unevolved conditions. Their main industries include farming, hunting, and fishing. Their living conditions are maintained by the income earned. Due to their financial difficulties, parents, therefore, encourage their kids to engage in income-generating hobbies. In this way, indigenous students face difficulties in their pursuit of education as a result of financial issues.

ii) **Management of Household Obligations:** In indigenous tribes, managing household responsibilities is typically done by children. They help their parents with a variety of home tasks, including gathering water, cleaning, washing, preparing meals, collecting wood products, raising livestock, and watching over younger siblings. Children are therefore prevented from attending school when they are urged to help handle household duties.

iii) **Less Parental Support in Academic Learning:** Parents should be involved in their children's academic learning as much as other people in the school, such as instructors and other students. In indigenous tribes, parental support is hardly ever present. The parents of the tribal youngsters are unable to assist them in completing their scholastic obligations. This is recognized as one of the biggest difficulties encountered during the educational process.

iv) **Low Levels of Motivation:** Students must be interested, enthusiastic, and highly motivated to achieve their academic objectives. Students from tribal backgrounds typically lack motivation. The main causes are poor comprehension of academic concepts, learning difficulties, a lack of learning resources, a lack of facilities and other infrastructure, and a lack of parental support, especially when it comes to academic learning. As a result, the students either have poor academic performance or quit school before honing their academic talents.

v) **Language and Cultural Barriers:** Language and culture are recognized as major obstacles that tribal students encounter while pursuing an education. Their prospects for a living are founded on the cultures, traditions, customs, beliefs, and principles unique to them. Additionally, they each speak a separate language. According to research, individuals have trouble establishing efficient communication channels with both professors and their fellow pupils because of linguistic difficulties. The process of learning academic concepts and achieving goals and objectives is significantly hampered by these variances.

vi) **Unsatisfactory Teaching-Learning Methods:** In tribal areas, schools either do not have enough teaching-learning methods accessible or the ones that are used do not meet the academic needs of the pupils. It is clear that if effective teaching-learning techniques are not used, students will undoubtedly encounter difficulties when they attempt to understand academic subjects. The curriculum's improper content and the use of a language that the tribal children are unfamiliar with as the medium of instruction are the main causes of inadequate teaching-learning methods.

vii) **Lack of Facilities and Amenities:** Facilities and amenities are lacking in tribal schools. The primary facilities required to improve the educational system include the right technologies, furniture, heating and cooling equipment based on the weather, clean drinking water, restrooms, library facilities, laboratory facilities, playgrounds, extracurricular and creative activities, and other supplies required to perform job duties suitably. In tribal schools, these amenities and facilities are not in a well-developed state. Therefore, this has shown to be a significant obstacle in the process of learning.

viii) **Lack of Learning Resources:** It is widely agreed that access to quality learning materials is essential to mastering academic concepts and achieving academic objectives. Students receive knowledge and information from them on a variety of topics and ideas. These consist of reading materials, technology, the internet, charts, models, posters, diagrams, and other visual aids. There is a dearth of educational resources for tribal students. They are unable to get enough educational materials because of their financial situation and poverty.

ix) **Participation in Income-Generating Activities:** Tribal groups typically live in impoverished and underdeveloped conditions. Their primary goal is to generate income so that they can maintain their living standards. Agriculture, farming practices, the manufacture of food items, handicrafts, artwork, and other such activities are the main sources of revenue for indigenous populations. Typically, the parents support their kids' involvement in jobs that pay well. Children, therefore, have difficulties in the process of learning when they are forced to help their parents in income-generating activities.

x) **Health Issues:** It's been said that indigenous communities rely on the environment's natural elements for survival. The tribal communities follow traditional practices and are not aware of current and advanced medical and healthcare treatments; instead, they obtain therapeutic herbs and plants from the forests in the event of any health issues or illnesses. They lack access to medical facilities or healthcare facilities because of their environmental circumstances. Tribal children's health issues are considered to be substantial barriers to their ability to pursue an education.

ix) **External Issues:** The approach taken for educational growth within tribal groups falls short of appropriately addressing the unique disadvantages that the tribal people possess. For instance, due to their small populations and erratic residence patterns, tribal places have not benefited from the population and distance guidelines established by the government. Furthermore, neither the tribal welfare department nor the education department has ever taken the time to fully comprehend the complicated realities of tribal life or the expectations that tribal members have of the system when developing policies and programs for tribal education. As a result, no useful policy for tribal education has been developed.

Internal Issues: The quality of schooling, the hiring of qualified teachers, the applicability of the curriculum and its contents, the medium of teaching, pedagogy, and special supervision are all examples of internal issues in tribal education. The vast majority of schools in tribal regions lack even the most basic infrastructure. Typically, schools in tribal communities have non-plastered floors, walls in disrepair, and thatched roofs. Schools in tribal areas hardly manage to operate with the barest necessities.

xiii) **Issues Concerning Teachers:** The villagers in tribal settlements hardly ever interact with the professors. The lack of accommodations for teachers in the hamlet causes them to be erratic and interferes with the regular operations of a school. Additionally, the value of education is diminished by the villagers' apathy and the hiring of inexperienced teachers in tribal communities.

xiv) **Parental outlook:** Tribal parents lack formal education. Their lack of literacy prevents them from comprehending the long-term benefits of schooling. Since schooling does not provide them with immediate financial benefits, parents prefer to place their kids in paying jobs that add to the family income and support the local economy. In addition, some parents who are now aware of the need for education choose not to provide it for their kids because they lack the means to do so.

xv) **Teaching Method:** In schools, instruction is conducted in English or regional languages. The indigenous people have distinct dialects that prevent their children from understanding what is taught in schools. The educational level of indigenous children is being lowered by this issue.

Suggestions:

The following are some ideas for enhancing tribal education:

1. The government should take specific action through various initiatives that can educate the indigenous people about the value of education, such as awareness camps, street drama, counseling, etc.

2. Teachers who are familiar with the local language and who respect and appreciate tribal customs and culture should be hired locally.

3. Infrastructure needs have always been disregarded. It needs to be taken into account. The necessary classrooms, instructional tools, electricity, water supply, separate restrooms for boys and girls, boundary walls, playgrounds, etc., should be provided for tribal schools.

4. To address the demand for skilled teachers, new teacher training facilities should be established in tribal sub-plan regions.

5. Instruction should be given in the regional tongue.

6. Courses that are career- or job-oriented should be prioritized.

7. Because there aren't enough higher secondary schools in tribal areas, the government must build residential schools there as part of several government initiatives.

8. There needs to be robust machinery in place to safeguard students from violence, exploitation, abuse, and neglect.

9. To raise awareness of the value of education, a proper awareness campaign should be established. To literate, the tribal, extensive literacy efforts may be launched as a matter of priority in the tribally dominant districts.

10. Through appropriate counseling and coaching, tribal parents' attitudes about schooling should be addressed.

11. All course materials should be available in the tribal peoples' native tongues.

12. Due to the low rate of higher education among the tribes, tribal students pursuing higher education, notably in the fields of medicine, engineering, and other vocational fields, should be given special ST scholarships.

13. Senior officials should regularly assess how well schools are run in terms of the curriculum, working hours, and attendance records.

14. Teachers must be motivated to do their best for tribal students in the classroom and made aware of their cultural and behavioral strengths. To recruit and keep qualified teachers in indigenous schools, incentives should be implemented. Only such driven teachers have a chance of engaging tribal students in their education.

15. More residential ashram schools are opening in the tribal areas to increase indigenous students' attendance.

Conclusion: Improving the economic and social conditions of the Scheduled Tribes requires a strong commitment to education. The development of a tribe depends on it. Children from tribal groups participate in and perform very poorly in educational programs in schools. For inclusive growth, there must be clear coverage for the use of local languages in classrooms. Although the tribes are improving in India, the pace of change has been sluggish. The state of tribal education could be a tale of sorrow, depression, and death if the government refuses to adopt a few drastic measures for its improvement. Therefore, it is now necessary to consider critically tribal education and inclusive progress. Therefore, to address this issue and increase funding in the federal and state budgets for tribal education, there is an urgent need for multiple government initiatives, planners, and policymakers. For indigenous children to join the mainstream of financial development, it is necessary to provide them with easy access and more chances. The indigenous people are extremely sensitive, and some of their issues are understood to be complex. The need of the hour is to preserve tribal traditions and ways of living in connection with nature for future benefit within human society.

CHAPTER SIX

TRIBAL DEVELOPMENT ISSUES AND CHANLLENGE

INTRODUCTION

In India, tribal people are mostly referred as Adivasis. They have been the most vulnerable community in India. Tribals are backward and poor and are mostly devoid of the common facilities like health, education etc. These societies did not follow the rules of Brahmins and had their own set of customs and rituals. Tribes are generally backward, economically as well as educationally. whereas in the mainland (central India) problems related to poverty, unemployment, indebtedness, backwardness, and ignorance ,social awareness are acute. The present paper is mainly based on secondary sources of data. The secondary data is also collected from various reference books, national & international research journal, magazine annual reports, and reports in Government, news paper & internet websites that helps in the tribal development issues and challenges. Education plays an important role in alleviating poverty in our community, society and tribals community. If a person is well educated, he can get a good job and earn money to support his family .It helps the society as well as the tribal community to move the country forward.

Whenever we think about tribal people the first thing that comes to our mind is the picture of half - naked men and women with some kind of weapon like arrows and spears in their hand and speaking in a cryptic language. When the majority of the community of the world kept pace with progress of the world there were communities still living in peace with nature with their traditional values, customs and beliefs. In India, tribal people are mostly referred as Adivasis. They have been the most vulnerable community in India. Tribals are backward and poor and are mostly devoid of the common facilities likc health, education etc. Since tribal communities in India have been materially backward and economically poor, some attempts have been made by the Government to develop them. Media also plays an important role in representing tribal communities. Since its inception it has played a central role because it is the single system through which public opinion could be stimulated. It also has a greater discourse that affects the policy-making process in a democracy. Despite that, tribal communities are still incredibly underrepresented in the media.

CONCEPT OF TRIBAL COMMUNITY

Indian history has witnessed various changes in society. Most of it encompasses the caste system followed religiously in our society. Apart from the social structure in the cities, there were other societies that flourished on the sidelines known as tribal societies. These societies did not follow the rules of Brahmins and had their own set of customs and rituals. Furthermore, they were also not divided into subclasses or caste, like other religions. These tribal societies were usually groups of people who had kinship bonds. These tribes were mostly involved in primary activities related to agriculture or animal husbandry. Some of them are also hunter-gatherers. Out of these tribal societies few tribes were also Nomadic. This meant that these tribes or groups of people move from one place to another and search for livelihood or other reasons. The settled tribal groups on the other hand had land and animals which they owned jointly as a tribe. The Tribe leader divided the animals and lands according to the needs and requirements of his people. These tribes were spread all across the country. Most of the tribes lived in forest Hills desert and far-fetched places. There are even shreds of evidence of tribal clashes amongst themselves as well as societies of other religions. The tribes continue to keep their freedom and culture separate from the rest of us. On one hand, they kept their societies separate from us but on the other hand, they were also dependent on us for their needs. We also traded in many handmade articles and wares from them. This led to a gradual change in both societies.

- Since the 1850s, these communities were loosely referred to as Depressed Classes, with the Schedule Caste and Scheduled Tribes.The early 20th century saw a flurry of activity in the British authorities assessing the feasibility of responsible self-government for India. The Morley–Minto Reforms Report, Montagu–Chelmsford Reforms Report and the Simon Commission were several initiatives in this context. A highly contested issue in the proposed reforms was the reservation of seats for representation of the Depressed Classes in provincial and central legislatures

- In 1935, Parliament passed the Government of India Act 1935, designed to give Indian provinces greater self-rule and set up a national federal structure. The reservation of seats for the Depressed Classes was incorporated into the act, which came into force in 1937. The Act introduced the term "Scheduled Castes", defining the group as "such castes, parts of groups within castes, which appear to His Majesty in Council to correspond to the classes of persons formerly known as the 'Depressed Classes', as His Majesty in Council may prefer".This discretionary definition was clarified in The Government of India (Scheduled Castes) Order, 1936, which contained a list (or Schedule) of castes throughout the British-administered provinces.

- After independence the Constituent Assembly continued the prevailing definition of Scheduled Castes and Tribes, giving (via articles 341 and 342) the president of India and governors of the states a mandate to compile a full listing of castes and tribes (with the power to edit it later, as required). The complete list of castes and tribes was made via two orders: The Constitution (Scheduled Castes) Order, 1950 and The Constitution (Scheduled Tribes) Order, 1950, respectively. Furthermore, independent India's quest for inclusivity was incident through the appointment of B. R. Ambedkar as the chair of the drafting committee for the Constitution. Ambedkar was a scheduled caste constitutional lawyer, a member of the low caste.

ISSUES THAT IMPACT ON TRIBAL EDUCATION

Some of the issues that impact the tribal education are as follows:

• Students: When they mingle with the rural/urban folks, the non-tribal schoolmates and even the teachers, who are normally outsiders, do not understand the tribal students.

• Teachers: Tribal students appear untidy, reinforcing their biases against tribal's. These biases are expressed in various forms of discrimination.

• Tribal youth: Tribal youths feel that teachers endeavor to undermine the attitudes toward their own customs, mannerisms, language, or, toward their cultural heritage in general.

• Society: General complain is that teachers did not teach them in the schools because they believed that if they did, the tribal students would no longer be dependent on them.

Solution

Some of the steps needed to take to improve tribal education:

• Need of educational bodies or non-profit that blend well with the tribal background and lifestyle

• Medium of instruction should be one that is familiar to them, and then gradually, they can be encouraged to take up regional languages

• Education should not be restricted to only learning but should evoke the responsibilities of the concerned individual towards his entire community

• Students should be taught to safeguard their own rights as well as the rights of their community and resolve to combat exploitation against their people

TRIBAL DEVELOPMENT ISSUES AND CHALLENGES

Tribes are generally backward, economically as well as educationally. The situation is not uniform in all parts of India. In the northeast, the situation has been disturbed for several years, whereas in the mainland (central India) problems related to poverty, unemployment, indebtedness, backwardness, and ignorance are acute.

The tribes of the northeast have a high level of politicization, literacy, and a high standard of living compared to their counterparts in other parts. The tribes were alienated from their own lands. The landlords and moneylenders of the plains gradually replaced the tribal landowners.

Some development issues and challenges of the tribal people are:

Loss of Control over Natural Resources

• Before the coming of the British, the tribal's enjoyed unhindered rights of ownership and management over natural resources like land, forests, wildlife, water, soil, fish, etc. With the advent of industrialization in India and the discovery of minerals and other resources in tribal inhabited areas, these pockets were thrown open to outsiders, and state control replaced tribal control.

• Thus began the story of unending miseries for the tribal's. With the impetus to the development process after independence, pressure on land and forests increased.

• This resulted in the loss of ownership rights over land, owing to chronic indebtedness, unscrupulous landlords, money¬lenders, contractors, and officials. With the concepts of protected forests and national forests gaining currency, the tribal's felt themselves uprooted from their cultural moorings and with no secure means of livelihood.

Poverty and Exploitation

• Poverty refers to the condition of not having the means to afford basic human needs such as clean water, nutrition, health care, clothing, and shelter. This is also referred to as absolute poverty. Relative poverty is the condition of having fewer resources or less income than others within a society or country or compared to worldwide averages.

• Generally, poverty is measured below Poverty Line (BPL) indices in rural areas. Below Poverty Line is an economic benchmark and poverty threshold used by the government of India to indicate economic disadvantage and to identify individuals and households in need of government assistance and aid. It is determined using various parameters which vary from state to state and within states.

• In the tenth five-year plan (2002-2007) survey, BPL for rural areas was based on the degree of deprivation in respect of 13 parameters, with scores from 0-4: landholding, type of house, clothing, food security, sanitation, consumer durables, literacy status, labour force, means of livelihood, the status of children, type of indebtedness, reasons for migrations, etc.

Displacement and Rehabilitation

• After independence, the focus of the development process was on heavy industries and the core sector. As a result, huge steel plants, power projects, and large dams came up—most of them in the tribal inhabited areas. The mining activities were also accelerated in these areas. Acquisition of tribal land by the government for these projects led to large-scale displacement of the tribal population. The tribal pockets of the Chhotanagpur region, Orissa, West Bengal, and Madhya Pradesh suffered the most.

• The cash compensation provided by the government was frittered away on wasteful expenditure. No settlements were provided for the displaced tribals within the industrial areas, who were forced to live in peripheries in slums or to migrate to adjoining states to work as unskilled workers in conditions of poverty. The migration of these tribals to the urban areas causes psychological problems for them as they are not able to adjust well to the urban lifestyle and values.

Lack of Awareness about Government Schemes

• In the Indian context, scheduled tribes have the special provisions, constitutional rights for their social, economic and educational promotion. Recent tribal welfare schemes are:

a) Pre-metric and post-metric scholarship for scheduled tribes students,

b) Boy's and Girl's hostel for the tribal students in the tribal-dominated areas.

c) Rajiv Gandhi National Fellowship Scheme for tribal students in higher studies,

d) Establishment of Ashram school in tribal subplan area,

e) Vocational training in tribal areas,

f) Adivasi Mahila Sashaktikaran Yojana

g) Tribal forest Dwellers Empowerment Scheme,

h) National Scheduled Tribes Finance and Development Corporation (NSTFDC) self-employment scheme,

i) Eklavya Model Residential School for tribal students,

j) Sikshasshree for tribal day scholars,

k) Old age pension scheme for tribal people from BPL families with age of 60 years or above

l) Development of particularly primitive vulnerable tribal groups etc.

Besides, there are other general social and economic developmental schemes.

In the field survey, it is found that most of the tribal people are very much poor, but they could not manage BPL ration card, job cards for 100 day works etc. Most of them hardly know the name of BPL ration card. As a consequence, they remain deprived from such benefits. Due to illiteracy and lack of awareness many families remain in dark about the assistance laid down for them by the Government. Government officers and supporting staff misbehave with them. More than 70% tribal households have no any banking facilities simply having no bank account.

Health and Nutrition

•The public health and nutrition of the tribal people were not satisfactory during the colonial rule. It was in the year 1912 the Dooars labour act was passed but it was concerned with government inspection only in the matters of sanitation and public health. The enactment was promoted by the high incidence of sickness resulting in absenteeism and heavy death toll among the workers due to various diseases, particularly malaria and blackwater fever. Even after the independence, the laborers had not been provided modern facilities of treatment.

•In most of the diseases were concerned, they had to depend on the local process of treatment by Ojha or kabiraj, apart from this they had to depend on charlatan or quack, as because there was no qualified doctor, as a result, the patients had to expire for the wrong treatment.

Man-Animal conflicts

•Wild animals were very common to wander through the thick jungles. But after thinning of jungles, In recent years the man-animal conflict has gone up steeply owing to the increase in human population; land use transformations, developmental activities; species habitat degradation and fragmentation; growth of ecotourism and also increasing wildlife population as a result of conservation strategies.

•The human population and its growing demands for land and biological resources affected this landscape to great extent. Fragmentation of habitat has primarily occurred as a result of infrastructure development, widening of the road, conversion of the railway line to broad gauge including heavy traffic, river training works through large scale construction of embankments, deposition of dolomite in rivers in the foothills bordering Bhutan, and particle-containing dolomite in the flowing river coming from Bhutan hills.

•Tea plantations have taken a heavy toll on adjoining grasslands and also the industry has produced a huge amount of unplanned human settlements. A decrease in appreciation and an increase in a negative attitude towards wildlife has serious detrimental potential to impact the natural system of coexistence. All these factors led to an increased level of human-animal conflict.

Physical Constraints

•Traditionally, tribal people are interested to live in remote places of jungles and mountains.

•Transportation and way of communication are very hard in a civilized society.

•Climate is not healthy mainly during the rainy season in many tea garden areas.

IMPORTANCE OF EDUCATION IN TRIBAL COMMUNITY DEVELOPMENT

Education helps a person to get knowledge and improve confidence in life. It can help you improve in your career and your personal growth. An educated person can become a great citizen in society. It helps you to take the right decisions in life. The modern, developed and industrialized world is running on the wheels of education. To be able to survive in the competitive world, we all need education as a torch that leads the way. Mentioned below are the various features of education which outline the importance of education in human life:

- **Safety Against Crime:** The chances of an educated person getting involved in crime or criminal acts are very low. An educated person is well aware of his/ her surroundings and is less susceptible to getting cheated or be fooled.
- **Women Empowerment:** The empowerment of women is an essential and important pillar to optimize the good functioning of our society and nation as a whole. We can break old customs like child marriage, sati, dowry, etc only by educating the men and women of our nation. The fundamental right of Right to Freedom and Expression can only be achieved if the women of our country are educated and empowered. We can win the fight against the many social evils.
- **Removing Poverty:** Education is pivotal in removing our poverty from our society and our country. The clutches of poverty are very harsh and one of the main factors behind all the problems of our society. If a person if well educated, he/she can get a good job and earn money to sustain his/ her family.
- **Preventing War and Terrorism:** Education teaches everyone the importance of peace and brotherhood. The importance of staying united and spreading love is the need of the hour. To achieve world peace and prevent war and terrorism, education is important.
- **Maintaining Law and Order:** A good political ideology can only be developed if the citizens of our country are educated and taught the importance of following and respecting the law and order of our country. Law-abiding citizens contribute majorly in improving and sustaining the law and order of the country and the world.

RESEARCH METHODOLOGY

The present paper is mainly based on secondary sources of data. The secondary data is also collected from various reference books, national & international research journal, magazine annual reports, and reports in Government, news paper & internet websites that helps in the tribal development issues and challenges.

REVIEW OF RELATED LITERATURES

1) S. Arya (2012) was conducted on A Critical Study of Tribal Education: With special reference to women.

The women in India, who were revered in ancient India but were the most neglected lots decades ago, have now been receiving increased attention. In India appreciable progress has been made in this direction- still much more remain to be done. Tribal society is far behind in education and in raising their social and economic status and thus integrating them in the so-called men dominated world of today. The large majority of population in tribal areas is backward due to the co-relation and least adoption of educational technology. The tribal societies are closed and isolated society living in compact groups. When this tribal groups are considered in case of educational field, the national average literacy rate in educational development among tribes is 29%, among which, the highest literacy rate of tribes is 36% in Gujarat (48% male and 24% female) and in Rajasthan literacy rate is just 19.44% (with female rate 4.22% and male rate 33.29%). To Some extent, education of this nature and pertaining to rural development has been attempted even before independence and as part of community development Block Programme. Here, However education has been limited to certain sectors and schemes, where extension services have been created primarily for execution of schemes prepared at the state or national level. Currently, a new dimension envisaged in the role of education in the developmental activities of the country. The economic co-relation and expectations from formal education have been correctly delimited to urban areas. While the extension of formal education to rural areas is expected to continue to provide coverage so as to ensure universal literacy and formal education. In such a situation the role of education for tribal develop becomes extremely significant. In India the government created so many policies and plans of education and development for tribal women's but there are so many problems also occurred to implement these policies

2) A . Gangele (2019) Studied on The Tribal Educational Status in India : Galore Challenges and issues . Education is the sole means to establish peace and unity in the world and education is the key to tribal development. The present study is to analyses status of tribal education with growth of education, literacy rate and gap between Scheduled Tribes and other social categories from the years to 2011, gross enrollment ratio, dropout rates and gender parity index in India. Along with this, it tried to highlight the status of tribal communities' education, the galore issues and challenges of play roles as an educational barrier. Tribal community in both rural and urban is facing various social and psychological problems in getting education. Educating tribals is not common task like educating non- tribals. They need special efforts by the government.

3) M. Mohan . kumar, V . k. Pathak , and M . Ruikar .was conducted on The Tribal population in India: A public health challenge and road to future. India with 8.6% of tribal population is finding it difficult to bridge the gap that exists between tribal and non-tribal population in regards to healthcare. Tribal population suffers triple burden of disease; in fact it is quadruple, namely, communicable diseases, non-communicable diseases, malnutrition, mental health, and addictions complicated by poor health seeking behavior. With increasing needs, an Expert committee on Tribal health has given recommendations with the goal to bridge the current gap in the health status of tribal people latest by the year 2027. An entirely parallel health system has been proposed with key focus areas, governance, and financing. To summarize and report the present scenario in terms of disease burden, health-seeking behavior, healthcare delivery system, and a roadmap for the future along the importance of primary healthcare in achieving it. Mere establishment of more health facilities cannot overcome the poor health of tribal population and so the role of trained manpower to deliver quality healthcare, in which case the role of traditional healers, local Tribal boys and girls comes in handy. It is high time and states should act swiftly to assess the needs, priorities of their own tribal population and set goals, targets to achieve the same through proven public health strategies.

4) Dr. R. K. Kaur (2020) Studied on "The Role of Education in the Empowerment of Tribal women"

The role of Education in the tribal women is at different levels of development. Earlier government had no direct programmed for their education, but in the subsequent years the reservation policy has made some changes. There are many reasons for low level of education among the tribal women. Formal education is not considered necessary to discharge their social obligations. Superstitions and myths play an important role in rejecting education. Most tribes live in abject poverty. It is not easy for girls to go to schools. As they are considered extra helping hands. The formal schools do not hold any special interest for the children. Most of the tribes are located in interior and remote areas where teachers would not like to go from outside.

FINDINGS

• Traditionally, tribal people are interested to live in remote places of jungles and mountains

- As a result, huge steel plants, power projects, and large dams came up—most of them in the tribal inhabited areas. The mining activities were also accelerated in these areas. Acquisition of tribal land by the government for these projects led to large-scale displacement of the tribal population.
- Poverty refers to the condition of not having the means to afford basic human needs such as clean water, nutrition, health care, clothing, and shelter.
- Due to illiteracy and lack of awareness many families remain in dark about the assistance laid down for them by the Government. Government officers and supporting staff misbehave with them.
- The high incidence of sickness resulting in absenteeism and heavy death toll among the workers due to various diseases, particularly malaria and blackwater fever.
- They had to depend on the local process of treatment by Ojha or kabiraj, apart from this they had to depend on charlatan or quack, as because there was no qualified doctor, as a result, the patients had to expire for the wrong treatment.

.CONCLUSIONS

The history of India has witnessed various changes in the society. Much of this revolves around the religiously practiced caste system in our society. In that religious society caste is divided into different levels. These caste societies did not follow the rules of the Brahmins, and their tribals community was one of them , had its own customs, cultures . Traditionally, tribal people are interested to live in remote places of jungles and mountains .As a result of being in a remote area, social norms could not be aware of the subjects. There are deprived of the continuity of society .The light of education does not reach them in the tribals community. Due to which the tribals community lags behind in social awareness. The tribal community of the society refers to poverty, the inability of people to afford basic necessities, conditions such as clean waters, health care, clothing and shelters, education. The grip of poverty is extremely severe and is one of the main reasons behind all the problems in our society. Wild animals have to struggle for habitat in the regional areas, in order to survive in daily life. Education plays an important role in alleviating poverty in our community, society and tribals community. If a person is well educated, he can get a good job and earn money to support his family .It helps the society as well as the tribal community to move the country forward.

CHAPTER SEVEN

TRIBAL EDUCATION IN INDIA: CHALLENGES AND SCHEMES

Introduction

Education is the sole means to meet the essential requirements for man-making and nation building. India is a land of diverse culture, religion, language and races. In the total population of India, tribal community is a small portion with their indigenous culture and language. Tribal community in India are geographically, socially isolated and economically marginalized and deprived in some way or the other. Education is a primary tool to uplift and empower the tribal community to overcome the barriers of their life. Sincere efforts were made for the economic and educational development of tribals in the post-Independence period. After Independence our constitution has laid down various schemes for the development of the tribal community. Inspite of various initiatives taken, the educational status of the scheduled tribes remains low. This paper analyses the status of tribal education, challenges and the various government schemes to promote education among tribals.

India has a rich glorious heritage, but a sizeable part of Indian population is yet to get benefits out of it. They are still tribal communities which are primitive and live in secluded areas (Verma 1996). The tribes in India usually reside in hill areas, forests, near the seas and in islands. Their lifestyle is quite different from non-tribals (Preet 1994). Since they are materially and economically backward, attempts have been made by the government to develop them. Today, the governments in all countries are paying special attention to development of the tribes (Nithya 2014).

Though our national leaders and constitutional makers are committed to uplift the tribal people, a desired level of development has not been achieved yet (Chandra Guru et. Al: 2015). In the light of above observations, the paper discusses the status, challenges in tribal education and schemes developed by the government for the tribal education in India.

1. Review of Literature

There is considerable literature on tribal development and growth of education among the tribals. According to Virginius Xaxa (2015), the colonial state did almost nothing to improve the socio-economic conditions of the tribals other than providing them protective measures. He says that the post-Independent India also continued the same policy with the little modification such as providing certain percentage of seats in state sponsored educational institutions and government services. Though reservation provides employment opportunities, the lack of educational qualifications and necessary skills denied them of the jobs, and the reserved seats remain vacant in many cases.

Gaurang Rami's (2012) paper discuss the status of primary education in tribal district of Dang in Gujrat. In the district, there are about 412 primary schools; out of which 378 primary schools are run by the district Panchayat. The conclusion is that most of the schools have buildings, but fail to attract the girl students owing to lack of other essential amenities like drinking water as well as separate toilets for boys and girls. Hence, the drop out ratio goes higher among the tribal girls. Another problem that makes tribal students leave schools is the medium of instruction which is quite different from their own vernacular dialect.

Pradhan and Sanjay Kumar (2011) describe that despite special initiatives like Ashram schools, introducing vernacular at primary level, and teaching in local dialects, the tribals are still lagging behind the non-tribals. Under such circumstances the government and policy makers should put best efforts to improve their educational status.

Arun Kumar Ghosh's paper (2007) provides in-depth literature on tribal education in Jharkand and West Bengal. He says that few tribals badly in need of special attention for literary and basic education. He observes the female enrolment ratio of the tribals is much lower among these tribals than that of their males. A further sharp decline of enrolment was observed immediately after the primary education, and this trend continued among males and females.

Vinoba Gautam's paper (2003) on Janasala experience, a collaborative programme between the government of India and United Nations agencies to achieve universal elementary education, especially for girls and children from the deprived communities, working children, and children with specific needs says that it tries to cover nearly three million children; out of it 33% would be tribal children. Finally, the paper concludes that non-tribal education has very limited value in tribal cultural milieu because it does not match with the lifestyle of individuals and the needs of the tribal community. There is a need to linking school education with life and the needs of the tribal communities.

Kumar Rana et. Al (2003), while reviewing the situation the situation of primary education in West Bengal, point out multiple problems that the primary education across India has been facing, such as infrastructure, shortage of schools, shortage of teachers and financial handicap of the parents. He also added that just identifying the problems of infrastructure would not provide quality or spread primary education.

3. Educational Status of Tribals in India

India advocates inclusive growth, but owing to lack of education and skill development, the marginalized sections are not becoming part of the inclusive growth. To ensure inclusive growth, the constitution has empowered the backward classes with reservations in education and jobs. For this purpose, the Constitution of India has earmarked certain provisions to enable the SCs and STs to access education (T. Brahmanandam & T. Bosu babu 2016). Framers of the Indian Constitution have paid attention to the marginalized section in India and listed the following constitutional provision for Scheduled Caste.

Article 46 of the Indian Constitution lays down that, the state shall promote, with special care, the educational and economic interests of weaker sections of the people, and particular, of the scheduled caste and scheduled tribes, and shall protect them from social injustice and all forms of exploitation.

Article 154(4) empowers the state to make any special provision for the advancement of any socially and educationally backward classes of citizen or for SCs or STs

Article 29(1) provides distinct languages script or culture. This article has special significance for scheduled tribes

Untouchability is abolished under Article 17, and its practice in any form a punishable offence

Article 275 (1) provides Grants in-Aids to states (having scheduled tribes) covered under fifth and six schedules of the constitution.

Article 350A states that 'It shall be the endeavor of every state and every local authority within the state to provide adequate facilities for instruction in mother-tongue at the primary stage of education to the children belonging to minority group.........."

Article 243D, 330 and article 332 provides reservation of seats for STs in gram Panchayat, house of people and state legislative assembly.

Many other provisions are laid down in articles 15,16,335,338A,342 etc.

4. Challenges in Tribal Education

Despite constitutional provisions educating tribal children is still a major concern for the government. There are so many socio-cultural, economical, geographical and administrative obstacles (report Ministry of Tribal Affairs, GOI, 2013) for which literacy rate of tribal people has never been at par with entire population, and gap between them is always high. The challenges faced by the tribal people in order to acquire education are as follows.

4.1. Language of Instruction

Language has been the important constraints in tribal education. Government schools use the state language for teaching, which is most often not familiar to tribal child at the pre-primary and primary levels. Tribal children have limited contact with the state language, and tend to speak in their home language. They are, thus, unable to fully comprehend classroom teaching and activities, read in the state language or understand the texts properly. But the study conducted by Pradhan and Pattanaik (2011) revealed that tribal students did not show interest to pursue formal education in their home language (s). They opined that education in the medium of their home languages (tribal languages) would not help them to expand the horizon of their knowledge.

4.2. Curriculum Content – Local Adaption of Methods and Materials

Research in child development and pedagogy has indicated that a young child learns concepts better if these are embedded in contexts that are meaningful, i.e. contexts that are local and familiar. The words, terminologies, messages, topics reflected in the syllabus and textbooks are most often alien to tribals (M.C.Upmanu 2016). The new National Curriculum Framework, however, recommends a plurality of textbooks meant to create a theoretical space for local specificity.

4.3. Teacher Training and Pedagogy

Teachers for educating children, in tribal/scheduled areas, may or may not be from the tribal community. The presence of tribal teachers, especially from the same community, has shown and improved school participation of tribal children, as these teachers understand and respect the culture with greater sensitivity. Training and capacity building has to be undertaken on a sustained basis to ensure continued motivation on the part of teachers. Studies suggest that teacher motivation contributes more to the teaching-learning process than teacher competence. The following are the key elements of teacher training and pedagogy:

- Training on Material Use
- Changes in perception of Teachers about Tribal Children
- Participatory Method of Teaching

In the absence of appropriate training in the use of materials, development of appropriate curriculum is a futile exercise. Research has shown that it is important to train the teachers in the use of dictionaries, flash cards and innovative teaching learning materials.

4.4. Community Participation and Ownership

For the community to be involved in the education process, youth tribal educators and tribal teachers from the community can act as agents of change. They can serve as role models and work together inside and outside the classroom. The following are key elements for effective community participation:

- **Obtain Buy-in from Local Stakeholders:** Gain trust of locals, learn from, and educate them, and build capacity of local tribal youths and community leaders.
- **Assure Community Participation:** Local community can participate and/or can be involved in different activities like construction of school building, documentation of local history, interaction between and amongst the participants through motivation.

- **Instill Sense of Accountability and Ownership among and Parents:** Local community should contribute in terms of cash, kind and labour, for the promotion of education of their children; and own the entire responsibilities of their school, including repair of school building, management of mid-day meal programme, preparation of TLMs, promotion of enrolment, school supervision and monitoring.
- **Empowering Communities:** Communities should be empowered to demand appropriate and quality education services from the government through a multi-pronged strategy. (Source: "The Tribal Education in India, Status, Challenges and Issues" by M.C.Upmanyu)

5. Schemes for Tribal Development

5.1. Tribal Panchsheel: Pandit Jawarhalal Nehru, the first prime minister of free India laid down five principles of tribal development which is called Tribal Panchsheel. It was ratified by Dhebar commission and enshrined in "A Philosophy for North Eastern Frontier Area" written by Verrier Elwin. These five principles are :

1. People should develop along lines of their own genius and we should avoid imposing anything on them. We should try to encourage in every way their own traditional arts and culture.
2. Tribal rights on land and forests should be respected.
3. We should try to train and build up a team of their own people to do work of administration and development. Some technical personnel from outside will, no doubt be needed, especially in the beginning. But we should avoid introducing too many outsider into tribal territory.
4. We should not over-administer these areas or over-whelm them with multiplicity of schemes. We should rather work through, and not in rivalry to, their own social and cultural institutions.
5. We should judge results, not by statistics or the amount of money spent, but by the quality of human character that is evolved. (Source : "A philosophy for NEFA" by Verrier Elwin)

5.2. Post-Matric Scholarship for Scheduled Tribe Students: This scheme was introduced to encourage the ST students pursuing Post-Matriculation, in professional, technical as well as non-professional courses in various recognized institution by providing them financial support. Students having family income not more than Rs. 10800 per year, are entitled for this scheme. This scheme is in operation since 1944-1942, and implemented by state government and UTs administration with 100% central assiatance.

5.3. Hostel for ST students girls' and boys' : A plan for providing hostel accommodation for ST girls' was started during third five years plan period and for the boys' this programme was launched in 1989-1990 and both these schemes merged in 10th five year plan. Aim of this scheme is to facilitate hostel accommodation to the peripheral ST students who are unable to pursue their education due to their financial condition and location of their residence.

5.4. Rajiv Gandhi National Fellowship Scheme (RGNF) : RGNF was introduced in the year 2005-2006 with the objective to encourage the students belonging to ST community to pursue higher education such as M.Phil and Ph.D by providing them financial assistance. University Grant Commission (UGC) took the responsibility to implement this scheme on the behalf of Ministry of Tribal Affairs.

5.5. Vocational Training Center in Tribal Areas: Aim of this scheme is to develop the skill of ST students depending on their qualification and present market trends. This vocational training would enable them to get suitable employment or enable them to become self sufficient.

5.6. National Overseas Scholarship Scheme for ST: This scheme provides financial support to those meritorious tribal students who wish to pursue their studies in abroad (Masters, Doctorate, Post-Doctorate) in specified field of Engineering, Technology, and Science.

5.7. Scheme of Top Class Education for ST Students: A scheme of scholarship was introduced by Ministry of Tribal affairs in 2007-2008 to encourage brilliant students of tribal community for continuing their study at degree or post-degree level.

5.8. Ashram School in Tribal Sub-Plan Area: This scheme was started in 1990-1991 with a view to provide education with residential facility to ST students.

5.9. Tribal Research Institute: Fourteen Tribal Institutes (TRIs) have been set in Andhra Pradesh, Assam, Bihar, Gujarat, Kerala, Madhya Pradesh, Maharashtra, Rajasthan, Tamil Nadu, West Bengal, Uttar Pradesh, Manipur and Tripura.

5.10. Book Bank & Coaching for ST: In order to reduce dropout rate among ST students from professional institutes/ universities, funds are allotted for purchase of books under this scheme. Also free coaching classes are provided to ST students to enhance their skill and capabilities for various competitive examinations, so that they can compete with main stream students in all competitive examinations. (Source: "Tribal Education in India: Government Initiative and Challenges" by Shyamal Kumar Daripa)

6. Conclusion

Education is an important avenue for the upgradation of economic and social status of marginalized communities in the society.Since the attainment of independence, government of India has planned several schemes to spread education among the tribals. Inspite of these schemes the education imparted to tribal communities does not meet its expected level. It is now significant that the time has come to consider the holistic tribal education and their inclusive growth. The government and policy makers need to concentrate more on a long-term strategy to enhance the educational status of tribal children. "Tribal communities will have to be elevated economically and educationally for promotion of a socio-economically integrated healthy society in the remote pockets," saidDaniel Pradhan, development practitioner who works with the Union Ministry of Minority Affairs. If drastic decisions are taken and effective plans are devised, the obstacles in pursuance of education by tribal children can be removed. Apart from government schemes, if various NGO's play a remarkable role in creating awareness among the tribals, the economic development of the nation can reach the desired height.

CHAPTER EIGHT

SOCIO-ECONOMIC, HEALTH AND EDUCATION STATUS OF TRIBAL WOMEN IN INDIA

Introduction

Approximately 8.2% of the country's population is made up of tribal people, or adivasis as they are more commonly referred to as a sign of self-assertion. The central region of India and some areas of the north-east are where the tribal people are primarily concentrated. It appears that women's status is significantly better in tribal societies than it is in society at large. In India in 1991, there were 971 females for every 1000 males in the tribes, compared to 927 females in the general population.

In the tribal community, women make up 50% of the total population. In comparison to women in general society, women's status in tribal societies is generally better. Indian tribal women are preparing the food in the village in Orissa, India. The Indian Constitution assigns special status to the Scheduled Tribes. Scheduled Tribes, also known as adivasis, vanbasis, tribes, or tribals, make up about 8 percent of the Indian population. There are 573 Scheduled Tribes spread across the nation, each of which speaks a unique language that differs from the one that is predominant in the State in which they reside. In India, there are more than 270 of these languages. In India, there are 74. 6 million tribal people, according to the 2001 census. Undivided Madhya Pradesh has the most tribal residents (16.40 million), followed by Orissa (7 million) and Jharkhand (6. 6 million).

From the Margins to the Center, a study recently released by Sama Resource Group for Women and Health (2018), focuses on health disparities among tribal communities in a few districts in Chhattisgarh, Jharkhand, and Odisha. The National Human Rights Commission (NHRC) supported it, and it vehemently emphasises the connection between tribal communities' poor health and their marginalised status in the socioeconomic and political contexts.

Some of the main causes of the marginalisation of Adivasis include land alienation, loss of access to and control over forests, forced relocation due to development projects and a lack of adequate rehabilitation, and debt.

Role of Education in the Empowerment of Tribal Women

In expressing his thoughts on education, Mahatma Gandhi said: "The fundamental problem is that most people don't understand what education actually entails. In the same way that we evaluate the worth of real estate or stock on the stock exchange market, we also evaluate the value of education. Only educational opportunities that would enable the help increase student income. We hardly ever consider ways to help educated people become better people. We argue that since the females do not need to work, they shouldn't receive an education. We have little chance of ever understanding the genuine benefit of education as long as these concepts are prevalent ".

In the current environment, education is very important. It is crucial because it serves as a pathway to knowledge, self-respect, and success in life. Additionally, it strengthened our morals, social skills, and character. It highlights a better citizen out of everyone of us since without information, man is nothing more than an ignorant beast.

What is education's purpose? When it should strive for equality, we divide and practise untouchability. dividing society into various castes. The women are expected to adopt their husbands' religion and don burqas.

Following marriage. At a very young age, we instil in kids the concept of caste inequality. We delegate

Boys and girls are treated differently at school, which causes them to feel unequal.

Given that women make up about half of the population of the country, women's education has special significance in the context of the country's growth. Education helps women develop fundamental skills and a value system that elevates their social status. In order to advance society, inclusive growth of

For this perspective, it is crucial to uplift the People who are Aboriginals, a primitive, uncivilised, indigenous, marginalised, and deprived segment of the community. All sections of the society are needed. The development of these towns is significantly behind schedule. They are a group of Indians who are socially, politically, economically, and culturally marginalised. One of the most undervalued groups in these Communities are the women.

Socio-Economic Status

She appreciates having the freedom to choose her marriage. A tribal woman can easily get a divorce and remarry. She has a job, so she is self-sufficient financially.

Women may wed more than one husband in some tribal communities. Polygyny is the practise of a man taking multiple wives. Polyandry is the practise of one woman having multiple husbands. They frequently use bride prices as part of wedding ceremonies. Surprisingly, in some tribal societies, the groom is required to perform physical labour and serve at the wife's home if he is unable to pay the bride price.

A tribal woman can easily get a divorce and remarry. She has a good job, so she is largely self-sufficient financially. Though the Socio-economic status of tribal women is very rich, their health and education status is that much poor in comparison to the national average.

Health Status of Tribal Women

Tribals have a very high infant mortality rate. Low health status in tribal women is caused by low nutritional status and a higher fertility rate.

In the tribal belt, a woman is regarded as healthy if she can have four or five children while also working in the fields.

The rural and tribal women in India encounter challenging health issues owing to a range of factors. Lack of access to quality healthcare, illiteracy, low socioeconomic status, nutritional deficiencies, and traditional beliefs are some of the contributing factors. Sexual and reproductive health are frequently harmed by extreme health neglect.

Tribal communities face the "triple burden" of disease. Apart from high rates of malnutrition and communicable diseases (TB, leprosy, HIV etc), the advent of rapid urbanisation, and changing lifestyles and environment, has led to a rise in non-communicable diseases as well (cancer, diabetes, and hypertension). These are both in addition to the burden of mental illness and subsequent addiction. In addition to this:

1. The reproductive health of women encompasses their holistic healthcare, including physical, mental, and social well-being.

2. Tribal women are mostly malnourished, and their daily intake of adequate nutrients continues to be much below the recommended standards. This has been a critical challenge adding to the health crisis in tribal regions.

3. The nutritional status of women reflects directly on their cultural practices and socio-economic situation. Malnutrition affects most women mainly during reproduction due to inadequate food consumption and lack of a nutrient-enriched diet.

4. Additionally, the cultural preference to bear sons results in a high fertility rate that is closely spaced. This leads to loss of nutrition from the body that can have an adverse impact during pregnancy and child delivery.

5. According to a study, women from rural areas between the age group of 15-24 years face a high risk of sexual and reproductive health outcomes, accounting for 41% of total maternal deaths.

Educational Status

Tribal women's low educational status is evident in their higher dropout rates, lower literacy rates, and lower school enrolment rates.

When considering the bigger picture, the low rate of literacy among tribal women across India serves as a stark reminder of the appalling situation facing STs in the nation. North-eastern states have led the way in embracing all STs, but the majority of large states are bewildered by the enormous literacy gap between all females and tribal women.

Tamil Nadu has a lot of catching up to do among the southern states. It stands out with the largest gap of 26.6%, according to the annual report of the Union Tribal Affairs Ministry, with the ST women's literacy rate hovering around 46.8%. lower than the 49.4% national average. The causes are widespread and include poverty, forced labour, early marriage, the absence of nearby schools, prejudice, and the indigenous population's nomadic lifestyle. With 71.1% and 53% respectively above the national average, Kerala and Karnataka stood out.

So what is the next step? State governments must implement programmes to bring tribal students into the classrooms and raise awareness of the value of education among STs, the majority of whom reside in distant villages. They should also implement the current Central programmes for ST students and make sure the money is distributed to those who are in need. Every school needs to monitor these students. Every citizen has a fundamental right to education, so using it as the main strategy to advance STs into the mainstream.

Literacy and Educational attainment is one of the important indicator of any country's level of human development. Education is essential for everybody irrespective of gender, caste, class, colour and creed , it is essential for both men and women. Education is a tool that enable women to find the right path for their overall growth and development. Even today in most of the States the tribal women are suffering due to blind beliefs, superstitions, orthodoxy and ignorance, though Scheduled tribe women and Girls are guaranteed Constitutional rights as well as rights under specific laws constituted by Parliament, especially for PESA(Panchayats (Extension to Scheduled areas) areas.

There are about 550 tribes in India. As per Census 1951, 5.6% of the total population of the country was tribal. According to Census 2011,the number of scheduled tribes in India is 10,42,81,034, which is 8.6% of the total population, where as, as per census 2001 the tribal population was 8.2%. During 2001-2011 the decadal growth rate of the population of India was 17.64%. During this period the decadal growth rate of the scheduled tribes was 23.7%. The decadal growth rate of the scheduled tribes in rural areas was less i.e 21.3% where as it was more i.e 49.7% in urban areas.

There has been a considerable increase in the literacy rates of tribals from 1961 to 2001 i.e 8.53 to 47.10. The Literacy rates among females also raised significantly during this period. Among the tribal women, living in urban areas there is nearly four fold increase in the literacy rates i.e. 13.45 in 1961 to 59.87 in 2001. Simultaneously the literacy rates among rural tribal women also increased from 2.90% to 32.44% during these four decades. This is due to the continuous efforts of the Government and Non government organisations towards educational development among Scheduled Tribes.

As per Census 2011, the rate of literacy in India is 72.99% whereas that of it in scheduled tribes is 59%. State-wise, the rate of literacy in scheduled tribes is highest in Mizoram (91.7%) and lowest in Andhra Pradesh (49.2%). Among union territories, the highest rate of literacy in scheduled tribes is in Lakshadweep (91.7%). The census 2011 data also indicate that some states with higher concentration of tribal population have been doing extremely well. They are Mizoram(91.5%), Nagaland(80.0%), Manipur(77.4%) and Meghalaya (74.5%). Where as some states with more number of tribal habitations continue to perform very low. They are Jharkhand(57.1%),Madhya Pradesh(50.6%),Orissa(52.2%),Rajasthan(52.2%) and Andhra Pradesh (49.2%).

The overall literacy rate of the Schedule Tribe in Odisha increased from 23.4% in 2001 to 41.2% in 2011. Despite this improvement, it remained lower than the national average which stood at 47.1 per cent.

Conditions of Tribal women in India

The tribal women, constitute like any other social group, about half of the total population. The tribal women, as women in all social groups, are more illiterate than men.Role of women is not only of importance in economic activities, but her role in non-economic activities is equally important. The tribal women work very hard, in some cases even more than the men.

- Mitra and Singh write that discrimination against women, occupational differentiation, and emphasis on status and hierarchical social ordering that characterise the predominant Hindu culture are generally absent among the tribal groups.
- Bhasin (2007) also writes that though tribes too have son preference, they do not discriminate against girls by female infanticide or sex determination tests.
- The status of tribal women can be judged mainly by the roles they play in society. Their roles are determined to a large extent through the system of descent.
- Most of the tribes in India follow a patrilinear system. There are exceptional cases like the Khasi, Jaintia, Garo and Lalung of Meghalaya in the North-East who follow the matrilineal system. The Mappilas of Kerala too are a matrilineal community.

Women in tribal communities put in a lot of work, so they are valued as assets. Unsurprisingly, they frequently pay a bride price during marriages. The tribal women in the North East were well known for their weaving abilities. The majority of tribal girls used to learn how to weave at home. Tribal women, as a result, have very little control over immovable property. They typically used to weave in their free time and for self-consumption. Land is rarely passed down to them, especially in patrilineal societies.

Problems faced by tribal women

1. Despite several economic, political and social changes, women, are still far behind.
2. Primitive Economy results in overburdening of women. They are exposed to wild animals, poisonous vegetation as a cost of survival (women are known to actively participate in economy)
3. Cultural Practices – Numerous practices like genital mutilation are disastrous to the physical and mental health of women.
4. Health: Malnutrition, anaemia, lack of access to healthcare & proper medicines, lack of literacy & education opportunities, low empowerment & sense of independence
5. Sexual Exploitation – A number of complaints regarding officials committing sexual offences have come to light. (especially Naxalite area)
6. Isolation – Prevents women to take up education or benefit from government policies like maternity benefit, reservation etc.
7. Financial exploitation by money lenders.
8. Male migration leading to feminization of agriculture and poverty.
9. Tribal migrant women face issues of low wages, bad work conditions, malnutrition, unhygienic sanitation, cramped housing.

Conclusion

Tribal feminism and philosophical feminism are divided in the West based on ideals. However, in states like Jharkhand, Chattisgarh, the seven sisters of the North East, Odisha, and others with a high concentration of tribal people, feminism is not divided by mere denomination but is instead unified by the ideology of achieving equality in both public and private spheres. There have been significant progressive changes in the tribal community in recent years after much deliberation. Both men and women are being impacted by modernization as it takes over. Men are still viewed as more deserving than women, however, because of the weight of unfair sociocultural norms and gender roles.and frequently by us as women. It's time to shine a spotlight on these tribal women and provide them with a stage to do so.

CHAPTER NINE

TRIBAL EDUCATION IN INDIA

Introduction

Education is one of the fundamental conditions for the creation of man. creating a nation. It is essential to human development. resources. Education transmits information, abilities, and character. After after independence, India's governments tended to prioritise literacy initiatives. putting a focus on the 3Rs (Reading, Writing, and Arithmetic) to meet expectations of the State Policy Directive Principles. In the New York City skyline The text attempts to be critical of education policy, which is likely to be discussed soon. to evaluate the data and level of education across Tribes globally India. It is not advisable to study development in isolation. Construction is not associated with the expansion of a small wealthy population. Like Amartya Sen According to (1999), unless human capabilities are appropriate In the current environment, education is very important. It is crucial because it serves as a pathway to knowledge, self-respect, and success in life. Additionally, it strengthened our morals, social skills, and character. It highlights better citizens out of every one of us since, without information, man is nothing more than an ignorant beast. What is education's purpose? When it should strive for equality, we divide and practise untouchability. The deprived conditions endured by marginalised populations are addressed and removed, but Development is not possible. He actually emphasised the abilities and freedom for humans, and this freedom can only be attained when the people

are granted political freedom, access to economic opportunity, and social security and openness. Despite the fact that these ailments are not the same another,India has a long and illustrious history, but a sizable portion of the population has yet to benefit from it. Still, these are tribal settlements,which are nomadic and occupy isolated areas (Verma 1996). Tribe is defined as "a collection of families possessing a common name, speaking a common dialect, and or purporting to occupy a common region and is not typically endogamous though initially it may have been so" in The Imperial Gazetteer of India, 1911. (Nithya 2014)

A number of factors, including poverty and illiteracy as two prominent ones, have contributed to the growth of tribal education, making it one of the most hotly debated policy problems in modern India. Due to their seclusion, accessibility issues, unfriendly environment, poor health, and superstitious beliefs, their educational standing has been deemed to be extremely bad and at its worst. Tribes should receive particular development assistance to improve their standard of living.

The key means of integrating the impoverished group and lifting them up is via education. Education will also impact a person's affluence, achievement, and sense of security in life. Education is more significant to the tribal people since it will enable them to understand their rights and maintain their history in their own unique ways.

Since India's declaration of independence, the federal and state governments have launched a number of initiatives and programmes to educate the nation's indigenous people. The creation of Ashram Schools, Ekalavya Model Residential Schools, Kasturba Gandhi Balika Vidyalaya, pre-matriculatory scholarships, and vocational training facilities are a few examples.

It has been the intention of policy analysts and educators to acknowledge the tribal children's innate learning capacity as well as their culture, language, and cognitive prowess. The country's tribal education system, according to their belief, might be modernised.

Education is crucial in the eyes of government planners for assisting indigenous peoples in adjusting to national integration. Their prosperity, success, and sense of security in life will also depend on their education. Tribes that continue to be either illiterate or irresponsible with regard to education will pay the price.

The Ministry of Tribal Affairs was established to guarantee a coordinated and planned approach to the development of scheduled tribes. Through residential schools known as ashram schools, the educational requirements of tribal students are largely met. The nation is home to 892 ashram schools that have received central approval. Up until they finish their secondary school, they offer boarding and lodging services to kids in indigenous territories. In addition to these, the department has begun 197 Ekalavya Model Residential Schools, which are modelled after KGBVs and Navodaya

Vidyalayas.

To guarantee comprehensive education in the tribal country side, however, a long journey must be travelled.

Objectives

- To explore tribal education and eliminate exploitation in rural locations.
- To make life better for tribal people by finding a proper healthcare facility and educational system.

Youngsters from tribal communities are educated differently than non-tribal children because of the quality of education in general. Being tribal, of course, entails that they are typically impoverished and reside in regions with low educational opportunities. Thus, the predicament is due to a number of interconnected problems rather than just the fact that they are tribal people. According to empirical research, tribal children have the fundamental cognitive skills and psychological traits necessary for effective involvement in school, and their poor accomplishment levels are explained by school-related factors just like they would be for non-tribal kids.

Internal variables, such as content and methodology, teacher absenteeism and attitude, language of teaching, incentives, and limited community ownership of education, are inherent to the structure of the education system and can be changed by suitable initiatives.

1. **Inadequate Educational facilities**

The indigenous people still lack the necessary educational facilities for their children's education, despite the government's attempts. The majority of tribal people reside in steep terrain, dispersed locations, inhospitable regions, and solitary settlements. It is still not entirely viable to give people access to education at their doorsteps with ease. Some areas have yet to develop an atmosphere that encourages all indigenous youngsters to pursue a decent education. Statistics show that owing to their lack of permanent structures, nomadic tribes and many tribal children living in remote locations are not able to attend school.

2.Education Language

Tribal youngsters typically talk in their native tongues since they have little exposure to the state language. During their first two years of school (classes I and II), tribal children have reportedly experienced language-related difficulties; they are unable to comprehend and interact with their classmates, prisoners, and instructors in regional language, which is their second language. At the pre-primary and elementary levels, government schools require students to learn and communicate in the state language, which is frequently unfamiliar to a tribal youngster. As a result, they are unable to completely comprehend the lessons and activities in the school, read in the official language, or comprehend the materials.

3. Differentiating viewpoint and profession

The attitude, perspective, work culture, level of life, and devotion to modernity of tribal tribes differ significantly when the entire tribal population is analysed. One set of tribes inhabits incredibly remote areas and has not yet seen civilization or integrated into society as a whole, abandoning their traditional methods of life and fashion. Another tribe that resides in towns and villages and is eager to benefit from the possibility of education is not yet given such facilities. A third group of tribal people coexist alongside non-tribal people in rural and semi-urban regions, make an effort to fit in with others, but are nevertheless disadvantaged owing to poverty, a lack of access to quality education, encouragement, etc. The fourth category of tribal people who have advanced in society owing to social mobility live better and more affluent lives than certain non-tribal people. Even though they are tribal, these four groups of people have diverse perspectives on life and education. Since the final category of persons does not require any particular therapy, as advised and implemented by the government, a comparable form of treatment for their elevation appears unsuitable. Additionally, the government has not implemented any plans for the development of the native settlements.

4. Local adaptation of teaching techniques and materials in the curriculum

The "relevant" culture of the community should be reflected in the educational curriculum. A young kid learns concepts more effectively when they are placed in relevant settings, which are circumstances that are local and familiar, according to research in child development and pedagogy. The majority of the time, the terminology, terminologies, messages, and themes included in the curricula and textbooks are foreign to indigenous people.

However, the new National Curriculum Framework suggests a variety of texts designed to develop a theoretical framework for regional distinctiveness. Workbooks are becoming more popular as a way to enrich education throughout the curriculum and motivate students to do homework outside of the classroom (e.g., conduct science experiments at home with local materials). Other educational tools that make learning more entertaining and imaginative include puppets, model making, singing and drama.

5. Psychology and Teacher Education

Teachers may or may not be from the tribal community while working with children in tribal or scheduled regions. Due to the instructors' higher sensitivity and understanding of the culture, the presence of tribal teachers—especially those from the same community—has increased and shown the school involvement of tribe students. Many states have appointed paraprofessionals or community instructors, assuming that indigenous teachers are a better match. Even if a teacher has tribal ancestry, they still need to undergo particular training in both course topics and acceptable behaviour with pupils from other tribes.

6. Widespread Poverty

Subsistence poverty is a serious problem for indigenous communities. They are neither lazy or uninterested in physical labour, but research has shown that their extreme poverty is caused by their ignorance and illiteracy. The majority of tribes still follow their ancient, archaic customs, which are now outmoded in the age of sophisticated science and technology. Despite having enough opportunity for free education supported by the State Government, parents do not take advantage of it owing to inadequate information and sensitization. Education and poverty cannot coexist in opposition.

7. Curriculum that is unpleasant and monotonous

Tribes have an own culture, tradition, set of values, manner of life, and way of carrying out activities. They find the curriculum that the School Board has set forth for use in the classrooms to be quite unappealing and uninteresting because they believe it does not adequately reflect their environment, beliefs, way of life, or feelings, and is also not in any way helpful to them in terms of earning and subsisting. Too many subjects that are not entirely required and valuable are included in the present curriculum. These kids therefore do not have a strong passion for learning the topics.

8. **Management and Involvement in the community**

Young tribal educators and tribal instructors from the community can be change agents in the process of involving the community in education. They can cooperate and act as role models both within and outside of the classroom. In addition, the nearby tribal community must be given the opportunity to participate in the project and feel truly invested in it. Always bearing in mind the community's changing demands, innovative and comprehensive methods of involving and/or soliciting participation from communities must be investigated.

Recommendations and Findings

Findings: -

- The majority of the areas have poor educational systems. The infrastructural resources and their accessibility are insufficient to meet the demands of education.
- There aren't many higher education institutions, but the lower level is adequate. As a result of the imbalance, many students—particularly female students—have to discontinue their studies in the middle of their studies.
- There is relatively little consistent attendance at these schools.
- These schools have an extremely high dropout rate, which is worse for some tribes and particularly for female students.
- The success percentage of pupils attending these institutions is not great, and this is especially bad for tribes.

Recommendations: -

- To encourage tribal education, literacy campaigns should be conducted in various tribal communities.

- Tribal pupils should be taught using pertinent study materials in their native tongues.
- Local area teachers and female teachers should be hired to schools in tribal communities.
- Different scholarships and stipends must to be offered to entice students to attend school.
- There should be residential schools in tribal areas to solve the transportation problem.
- There should be careful monitoring to ensure that the tribes' plans are implemented correctly and that the teachers are acting honestly in their roles.
- The operation of the school should be routinely examined by a senior authority.

Conclusion

Education is the single most crucial tool for helping people and society increase their ability, get over obstacles, and have more chances for their well-being. Finding a balance between maintaining tribal cultural identity and mainstreaming appears vital in the context of ST children's education. It entails creating educational plans that guarantee an indigenous child's success in regular classrooms. The existing educational system is evidently primarily intended for the dominant group. As a result, funding must be allocated to developing support systems that serve as an addition to indigenous children's formal education system integration.

In the educational system, there may be the following support:

- Speaking tribal and official languages simultaneously in the pre-primary and elementary grades.
- Producing supplemental, pertinent learning resources for tribe members.
- Providing financial and non-financial incentives to instructors in indigenous territories.
- Attending to the health and dietary requirements of indigenous children.
- Increasing community involvement through teacher and youth training for indigenous members.
- Opening up transitional schools with an emphasis on integrating indigenous children.

- Establishing residential schools and temporary accommodations specifically for children of migrant workers.

Some of the problems that indigenous children have in the classroom are addressed through the support systems mentioned above. However, it is clear that additional philanthropic investment is needed outside of the classroom based on the examination of the reasons causing non-enrolment and/or dropout as well as case study descriptions. This would offer a firm foundation that makes the most of these resources and fosters the development of stronger individualised potential that can overcome the current constraints faced by tribe members.

Education at all levels, from primary school to technical college, has the power to unite humanity on a single platform where individual potential and competence determine the value of life. The platform for growth is where India's vision and the globalisation race's competitive difficulties meet. Abuse of human rights is "normal" in the majority of our nations. There have been several murders, mutilations, and tortures. The authorities use force to disperse peaceful protests. In most nations, there is ample evidence that is plain to observe. Most of our nations' judicial systems are deficient in the necessary impartiality and independence. Judges who refuse to pander to the whims and fancies of the ruling regime are either fired or mysteriously killed. The majority of criminal offenders receive unfair trials in court, and many unfortunate persons are detained even without being charged. Political rivals are frequently the victims of this violation of human rights. The majority of governments in our region of the globe control the state press and electronic media, as well as the decision of which news items will be published or transmitted. The parties on the other side of the political spectrum are frequently barred from using these facilities without restriction. They are always viewed as political rivals rather than potential future regimes. Our cities are teeming with street kids who spend their days sleeping on verandahs and kiosks, not knowing where their next meal will come from, due to the exorbitant expense of schooling, poverty, and a lack of supplies and (school) buildings.

CHAPTER TEN

CONSTITUTIONAL PROVISIONS FOR INDIAN TRIBES: A THEORETICAL ASPECTS

Introduction:

The framers of the Constitution took note of the fact that certain communities in India were suffering from extreme social, educational and economic backwardness. They needed special consideration for safeguarding their interests and for their socio-economic development. The Indian Constitutional Law is a philosophical legal document. Constitutional provisions are living instruments to safeguard the interests of people in general and special provisions for tribal people in particular. On the ground of special Constitutional provisions are not a discrimination, but it's protective discrimination that is indispensable for tribal development in India. The aimed to special provisions for prevent discrimination against the tribal people to protect their rights and make easy to maintain lifestyle. It improves the standard of living of tribal people in a socially, politically and economically back to return our mainstream of the Indian society. The National Commission for Tribal and Ministry of Tribal Affairs are the leading organizations to provide and implement various schemes and policies for safeguard the life of the tribal people with a view to protecting them from social injustice, discrimination, untouchablity and all forms of physical or mental exploitation. The aims and objectives of this paper to focus on the constitutional provisions for tribal safeguards and their development in India and indicated also the present situation and scenario.

The tribes are the native people of the land, who are believed to be the earliest settlers in the Indian Peninsula. They are generally called 'Adivasi', implying original inhabitants. The ancient and medieval History mentions a large number of tribes living in India. The framers of the Indian constitution with their prescience provided special status for socio-economic development of tribal people. Many laws, schemes, project and policy - programme has been created to bring the tribal people to the main stream of an ideal democratic set up for living a suitable society. The tribal law and administration provides not only constitutional safeguards and privileges but also provides the legal benefits to the tribal people. The Constitution of India and our basic structure of The preamble of India focused to all its citizens like social and economic justice, equality of status and opportunity and assures the dignity of the individual. All fundamental rights available to the citizens of India, any order and legislation of the Government and also equally available to the tribal community. The Constitution of India has several provisions to prevent discrimination against the people those are belonging to scheduled tribes and to protect their rights. The Government of India declare lots of resources to improve the standard of living of tribal people and also helped them through legislations, administration, developmental and many special programmes for safeguarding their rights and life.

The aims and objectives of this paper to focus on the constitutional provisions for tribal safeguards and their development in Indian society and coming back to a normal lifestyle in others people's of our society in the present situation and scenario.

Definition & Attributes of Tribes:

The term 'Scheduled Tribes' first appeared in the Constitution of India. Article 366 (25) of the Constitution of India defined scheduled tribes as "such tribes or tribal communities or parts of or groups within such tribes or tribal communities as are deemed under Article 342 to be Scheduled Tribes for the purposes of this constitution". Article 342 prescribes the procedure to be followed in the matter of specification of scheduled tribes. The President may, with respect to any State or Union territory, and where it is a state, after consultation with the Governor thereof by public notification, specify the tribes or tribal communities or parts of or groups within tribes or tribal communities which shall, for the purposes of this constitution, is deemed to be scheduled tribes in relation to that state or Union Territory, as the case may be. Parliament may by law include in or exclude from the list of Scheduled tribes specified in a notification issued under clause(1) any tribe or tribal community or part of or group within any tribe or tribal community, but save as aforesaid, a notification issued under the said clause shall not be varied by any subsequent notification. Thus, the first specification of Scheduled Tribes in relation to a particular State/ Union Territory is by a notified order of the President, after consultation with the State governments concerned. These orders can be modified subsequently only through an Act of Parliament.

The tribal communities in India have been recognized by the Indian Constitution under 'Schedule 5' of the constitution. Hence the tribes recognized by the Constitution are known as 'Scheduled Tribes'. Article 366 (25) defined scheduled tribes as "such tribes or tribal communities or parts of or groups within such tribes or tribal communities as are deemed under Article 342 to be Scheduled Tribes for the purposes of this constitution". Specification of a community as Scheduled Tribes (ST)The criterion followed for specification of a community, as scheduled tribes are indications of primitive traits, distinctive culture, geographical isolation, shyness of contact with the community at large, and backwardness. This criterion is not spelt out in the Constitution but has become well established.

A criterion being followed is based on certain attributes such as; a). Geographical isolation - They live in cloister, exclusive remote and inhospitable areas like hills, forests, b).Backwardness- Livelihood based on primitive agriculture, low cost closed economy based on low level of technology which leads to their poverty. They have a low level of literacy and health. c). Distinctive culture, language and religion they have developed community wise their own distinctive culture, language and religion. d). Shyness of contact – they have margin degree of contact with other cultures and people.

Protective & Developmental Safeguards:

The term Protective means here the reservation of the seats, for maintain the equal status and position for tribal people. These protections indicate their normal lifestyle in our Indian social streams.

National Commission for Scheduled Tribes:-

The National Commission for Scheduled Tribes was established by amending Article 338 and inserting a new Article 338A in the Constitution through the Constitution Act, 2003. By this amendment, the erstwhile National Commission for Scheduled Castes and Scheduled Tribes was replaced by two separate Commissions namely- (i) the National Commission for Scheduled Castes and (ii) the National Commission for Scheduled Tribes in 19 February 2004. The National Commission for Scheduled Tribes has a Chairperson, a Vice-Chairperson and three other Members. At least one other Member shall be appointed from amongst women. The Chairperson, Vice-Chairperson and other Members of the Commission are appointed by the President by warrant under his hand and seal. The Chairperson, the Vice-Chairperson and the other Members shall hold office for a term of three years from the date on which he or she assumes such office. The Chairperson has been given the rank of Union Cabinet Minister, and the Vice-Chairperson that of a Minister of State and other Members have the ranks of a Secretary to the Government of India.

The Duties assigned to the Commission under 338A are as ; (a) To investigate and monitor all matters relating to the safeguards provided for the Scheduled Tribes under the Constitution or under any other law for the time being in force or under any order of the Government and to evaluate the working of such safeguards; (b)To inquire into specific complaints with respect to the deprivation of rights and safeguards of the Scheduled Tribes; (c)To participate and advise in the planning process of socio-economic development of the Scheduled Tribes and to evaluate the progress of their development under the Union and any State; (d)To present to the President, annually and at such other times as the Commission may deem fit, reports upon the working of those safeguards; (e)To make in such reports, recommendations as to the measures that should be taken by the Union or any State for effective implementation of those safeguards and other measures for the protection, welfare and socio-economic development of the Scheduled Tribes. There are various laws and regulation are passed by the Indian Parliament for the protection of the life and also safeguard to maintain the daily lifestyle of ST peoples.

Agency for monitoring safeguards:

(1) There shall be a Commission for the Scheduled Tribes to be known as the National Commission for the Scheduled Tribes.

(2) Subject to the provisions of any law made in this behalf by Parliament, the Commission shall consist of a Chairperson, Vice-Chairperson and three other Members and the conditions of service and tenure of office of the Chairperson, Vice-Chairperson and other Members so appointed shall be such as the President may be rule determine.

(3) The Chairperson, Vice-Chairperson and other Members of the Commission shall be appointed by the President by warrant under his hand and seal.

(4) The Commission shall have the power to regulate its own procedure.

Directive Principles of State Policy:

Part IV of the Indian Constitution ensure that, the State shall promote with special care the educational and economic interests of the weaker sections of the people in particular, of the Scheduled Castes and the Scheduled Tribes, and shall protect them from social injustice and all forms of exploitation. Claims of Scheduled Castes and Scheduled Tribes to services and posts.The claims of the members of the Scheduled Castes and the Scheduled Tribes shall be taken into consideration, consistently with the maintenance of efficiency of administration, in the making of appointments to services and posts in connection with the affairs of the Union or of a State; Provided that nothing in this article shall prevent in making of any provision in favour of the members of the Scheduled Castes and the Scheduled Tribes for relaxation in qualifying marks in any examination or lowering the standards of evaluation, for reservation in matters of promotion to any classes of services or posts in connection with the affairs of the Union or State.

Reservation of seats in state Legislature :

1. Seats shall be reserved for the Scheduled Castes and the Scheduled Tribes, except the Scheduled Tribes in the autonomous districts of Assam, in the Legislative Assembly of every State.

2. Seats shall be reserved also for the autonomous districts in the Legislative Assemble of the State of Assam.

3. The number of seats reserved for the Scheduled Castes or the Scheduled Tribes in the Legislative Assembly of any State under clause (1) shall bear, as nearly as may be, the same proportion to the total number of seats in the Assembly as the population of the Scheduled Castes in the State or of the Scheduled Tribes in the State or part of the State, as the case may be, in respect of which seats are so reserved bears to the total population of the State.

(4) The number of seats reserved for an autonomous district in the Legislative Assembly of the State of Assam shall bear to the total number of seats in that Assembly a proportion not less than the population of the district bears to the total population of the State.

(5) The constituencies for the seats reserved for any autonomous district of Assam shall not comprise any area outside that district.

(6) The reservation of seats for the Scheduled Castes and the Scheduled Tribes in the House of the People and in the Legislative Assemblies of the States; and

Developmental Administration in Grassroots level:

- Seats shall be reserved for the Scheduled Castes; and the Scheduled Tribes in every Panchayat and the number of seats reserved shall be the same proportion to the total number of seats to be filled by direct election in that Panchayat as the population of the Scheduled Castes in that Panchayat area or the Scheduled Tribes in that Panchayat area bears to the total population of that area and such seats may be allotted by rotation to different constituencies in a Panchayat.

- Not less than one-third of the total number of seats reserved under clause (1) shall be reserved for women belonging to the Scheduled Castes or as the case may be, the Scheduled Tribes.

- Not less than one-third (including the number of seats reserved for women belonging to the Scheduled Castes and the Scheduled Tribes) of the total number of seats to be filled by direct election in every Panchayat shall be reserved for women and such seats may be allotted by rotation to different constituencies in a Panchayat.

- The offices of the Chairpersons in the Panchayats at the village or any other level shall be reserved for the Scheduled Castes, the Scheduled Tribes and women in such manner as the Legislature of a State may, by law, provide: Provided that the number of offices of Chairpersons reserved for the Scheduled Castes and the Scheduled Tribes in the Panchayats at each level in any State shall bear, as nearly as may be, the same proportion to the total number of such offices in the Panchayats at each level as the population of the Scheduled Castes in the State or of the Scheduled Tribes in the State bears to the total population of the State: Provided further that not less than one-third of the total number of offices of Chairpersons in the Panchayats at each level shall be reserved for women: Provided also that the number of offices reserved under this clause shall be allotted by rotation to different Panchayats at each level.

- The reservation of seats under clauses (1) and (2) and the reservation of offices of Chairpersons (other than the reservation for women) under clause (4) shall cease to have effect on the expiration of the period specified in article 334.

- Nothing in this Part shall prevent the Legislature of a State from making any provision for reservation of seats in any Panchayat or offices of Chairpersons in the Panchayats at any level in favour of backward class of citizens

On the other side development of tribal people by our urban administration, as;

1. Seats shall be reserved for the Scheduled Castes and the Scheduled Tribes in every Municipality and the number of seats so reserved shall bear, as nearly as may be, the same proportion to the total number of seats to be filled by direct election in that Municipality as the population of the Scheduled Castes in the Municipal area or of the Scheduled Tribes in the Municipal area bears to the total population of that area and such seats may be allotted by rotation to different constituencies in a Municipality.

2. Not less than one-third of the total number of seats reserved under clause (1) shall be reserved for women belonging to the Scheduled Castes or, as the case may be, the Scheduled Tribes.

3. Not less than one-third (including the number of seats reserved for women belonging to the Scheduled Castes and the Scheduled Tribes) of the total number of seats to be filled by direct

Election in every Municipality shall be reserved for women and such seats may be allotted by rotation to different constituencies in a Municipality.

4. The offices of Chairpersons in the Municipalities shall be reserved for the Scheduled Castes, the Scheduled Tribes and women in such manner as the Legislature of a State may, by law, provide.

5. The reservation of seats under clauses (1) and (2) and the reservation of offices of Chairpersons (other than the reservation for women) under clause (4) shall cease to have effect on the expiration of the period specified in article 334.

6. Nothing in this Part shall prevent the Legislature of a State from making any provision for reservation of seats in any Municipality or offices of Chairpersons in the Municipalities in favour of backward class of citizens.

ARTICLE 15 (Social Development): Prohibition of discrimination on grounds of religion, race, caste, sex or place of birth—

(1) The State shall not discriminate against any citizen on grounds only of

religion, race, caste, sex, place of birth or any of them, .

(2) No citizen shall, on grounds only of religion, race, caste, sex, place of birth or any of them, be subject to any disability, liability, restriction or condition with regard to—

(a) Access to shops, public restaurants, hotels and places of public entertainment; or

(b) The use of wells, tanks, bathing Ghats, roads and places of public resort maintained wholly or partly out of State funds or dedicated to the use of general public.

(3) Nothing in this article shall prevent the State from making any special provision for women and children.

(4) Nothing in this article or in clause (2) of article 29 shall prevent the State from making any special provision for the advancement of any socially and educationally backward classes of citizens or for the Scheduled Castes and the Scheduled Tribes.

ARTICLE 16: (Service & Employment Safeguard); Equality of opportunity in matters of public employment—

(1) There shall be equality of opportunity for all citizens in matters relating to

employment or appointment to any office under the State.

(2) No citizen shall, on grounds only of religion, race, caste, sex, descent, place of birth, residence or any of them, be ineligible for, or discriminated against in respect of, any employment or office under the State.

(3) Nothing in this article shall prevent Parliament from making any law prescribing, in regard to class or classes of employment or appointment to an office prior to such employment or appointment.

(4) Nothing in this article shall prevent the State from making any provision for the reservation of appointments or posts in favour of any backward class of citizens which, in the opinion of the State, is not adequately represented in the services under the State.

Suggestions:

The makers of the Indian Constitution were concerned and alert about the problems of tribes. Article 32 of the Constitution provides the right to Constitutional remedies. All the Articles discussed in the content are in favour of tribe preservation, safeguard and socio-economic upliftment and development. The framers of the Constitution wanted to build an egalitarian Indian society through these writings. Both the Central and State government have responsibility to take measure for wellbeing of tribes and towards that create social consciousness. At the present situation, tribal people are not even able to demand their rights due to poor and unconscious response of the authorities. Above all the authorities claim their rights, they are asked to produce certain documents which they generally do not have and they fall prey to corruption. The implementation of Government action and activity are very poor, for the result of suffering the tribals. So top to bottom each and every action should be taken very fast and smoothly due to tribal development. We are being very hopeful to full fill every desire to the Tribals.

References

- THE HISTORY OF TRIBAL ADMINISTRATION, https://egyankosh.ac.in/bitstream/123456789/71393/1/Unit-4.pdf
- Tribal Uprisings in the 18th and 19th Centuries, https://unacademy.com/content/mppsc/study-material/history/tribal-uprisings-in-the-18th-and-19th-centuries/
- Tribals and Tribal Policy, https://journalsofindia.com/tribals-and-tribal-policy/, December 4, 2018
- The authors are C. von Fürer-Haimendorf and E. von Fürer-Haimendorf. (2021). The Gonds of Andhra Pradesh: Indian tribal heritage and change. Routledge.
- the following individuals: Chaubey, G., Tamang, R., Pennarun, E., Dubey, P., Rai, N., Upadhyay, R. K.,... & R. Villems (2017). Reconstructing the demographic history of the Dravidian-speaking Gond, the biggest tribe in India. 25(4), 493-498, European Journal of Human Genetics.
- B. Sinha. (2017). Life, livelihood, and educational opportunities for the Maharashtrian Katkari tribes. 6, 57–64, Indian Journal of Educational Research.
- S. C. Verma (2010). A study of sociocultural dynamics, The Eco-friendly Tharu Tribe. Asian and Pacific Studies Journal, 1 (2).
- S. C. Verma (2010). A study of sociocultural dynamics, The Eco-friendly Tharu Tribe. Asian and Pacific Studies Journal, 1 (2).
- Gordon E. Dobson (1875). about the Andaman Islands and Andamanese. Journal of the British and Irish Anthropological Institute, 4, 457-467.
- Akula, S. (2013). Education for Children of Tribal Community- A Study of Adilabad District. American International Journal of Research in Humanities, Arts and Social Sciences, 4(2), 192-196. Retrieved from http://iasir.net/AIJRHASSpapers/AIJRHASS13-377.pdf
- Andrabi, A. A. & Jabeen, N. (2018). Scheduled Tribes Education in India: Issues and Challenges. Scholarly Research Journal for Interdisciplinary Studies, 5(45), 10738-10747. Retrieved from http://www.srjis.com/pages/pdfFiles/15337177379.%20Dr.%20Azad%20Ahmad%20Andrabi.pdf

REFERENCES

- Arya, S. & Chauhan, T. (2012). A critical study of tribal education: with special reference to women's. Retrieved from https://www.researchgate.net/publication
- Abdulraheem, A. (2011) Education for the Economically and Socially Disadvantaged Groups in
- India: An Assessment Economic Affairs Vol. 56 No. 2 June 2011 (Page 233-242)
- Basumatary, M. (2020). Issue, Challenge and Development Problems in Socio, Economic and Culture of Tribal People in Assam. International Journal of Recent Technology and Engineering, 8(5), 5222-5224. Retrieved from https://www.ijrte.org/wp-content/uploads/papers/v8i5/D9226118419.pdf
- Daripa, S. K. (2017). Tribal Education in India : Government Initiative and Challenges. International Journal of Research in Social Sciences. 7(10), 156-166. Retrieved from https://www.ijmra.us/project%20doc/2017/IJRSS_OCTOBER2017/IJMRA-12325.pdf
- Jha, J., Jhingran, D. (2002), Elementary Education for the Poorest and Other Deprived Groups,
- Centre for Policy Research. New Delhi.
- Lal, M. (2005), Education-The Inclusive Growth Strategy for the economically and socially
- disadvantaged in the Society
- Nair, P. (2007), "Whose Public Action? Analyzing Inter-sectoral Collaboration for Service
- Delivery: Identification of Programmes for Study in India."International Development Department, Economic and Social Research Council.February.
- Kapur, R. (2019). Problems in Tribal Education. Retrieved from https://www.researchgate.net/publication/ 334479483_Problems_in_Tribal_Education/link/ 5d2d805d299bf1547cb9e43c/download
- Mukherjee, A. (2009). Tribal Education in India: An Examination of Cultural Imposition and Inequality. (MA Thesis, Kansas State University Manhattan, Kansas). Retrieved from https://krex.k-state.edu/dspace/ bitstream/handle/2097/1520/ AnirbanMukherjee2009.pdf?sequence=1&isAllowed=y
- Sahu, K. K. (2014). Challenging Issues of Tribal Education in India. IOSR Journal of Economics and Finance, 3(2), 48-52. Retrieved from

REFERENCES

https://www.iosrjournals.org/iosr-jef/papers/vol3-issue2/Version-2/J03224852.pdf

- Sahu, K. K. (2014). Myths and Realities of Tribal Education: A Primary Study in Similipal Area of Odisha. International Journal of Humanities and Social Science Invention, 3(4), 1-6. Retrieved from http://www.ijhssi.org/papers/v3(4)/Version-1/A03410106.pdf

- Satyasavitri, V. B. & Honakeri, P. M. (2018). Impact of Ashram Schools Issues and Challenges of Tribal Education in India. International Journal of Scientific and Research Publications, 8(2), 475-478. Retrieved from http://www.ijsrp.org/research-paper-0218/ijsrp-p7459.pdf

- Singha, R. (2019). Responsible factors behind tribal primary education: a study in Bamongola and Habibpur Block of Malda District, West Bengal. Ensemble, 1(1), 57-62.

- Sedwal, M. & Sangeeta, K. (2008) Education and Social Equity with special focus on Scheduled Castes and Scheduled Tribes in Elementary Education,NUEPA, New Delhi

- Sujatha, K. (2002) Education among Scheduled Tribes. In Govinda, R. (ed.), India Education Report: A Profile of Basic Education. New Delhi: Oxford University Press.

- Kaur. K. R. (2020) " Role of Education in the Empowerment of Tribal Women" . Vol-6 issue. 2020.

- Mohanty. A. (2020) " Education for Tribals : Bottlenecks and the way forward " http://www.downtoearth.org.in

- Heredia . C. R. (1995) " Tribal Education for development : Need for a liberative pedagogy for social Transformation " Economic and political weekly vol. 30 No. 16 PP. 891-893+895-897 (6 Pages) http://www.juster.org. stable/4402663.

- Roy .P. (2021) " NEP and The education of Tribal children " http://www.smilefoundationindia.org.

- Marfatia . A (2018) " India's First Comprehensive. Tribal health report ". http://www.idronline.org.

- http://www.en.wikipedia.org.

- Arya.S. (2012) " A Critical Study of Tribal Education with special reference to Women" . http://www.Researchgate.net.

- Gangele. A. (2019) "The Tribal Education Status in India : Galore Challenges and issues " http://www.jetir.org.

- Kumar. M. M , Pathak .V. k, and Ruikar. M. (2020) " Tribal Population in India : A Public health challenge and road to future" .

http://www.ncbi,nlm,nih.gov.

- Abhisek Basu, S. C. (2014). Status of educational performance of tribal students: a study in Paschim Medinipur District, West Bengal. Retrieved from Academic Journals: https://academicjournals.org/journal/ERR/article-full-text/884A4B747828
- Bhuriya, M. (1985). Tribal Education in India. Retrieved from Cultural Survival: https://www.culturalsurvival.org/publications/cultural-survival-quarterly/tribal-education-india
- Digambar Naik, R. G. (2020). Tribal Education: Challenges And Ongoing Measures A Critical Analysis. Retrieved from Ilkogretim Online: https://www.ejmanager.com/mnstemps/218/218-1650468552.pdf?t=1659035008
- International, S. (n.d.). Educating the Tribal Children. Retrieved from Sewa International: https://sewausa.org/educating-the-tribal-children#
- Mandir, S. (2020). Help rural tribal children access education. Retrieved from Give India: https://www.giveindia.org/program/help-rural-tribal-children-access-education
- Mohanty, A. (2020). Education for tribals: Bottlenecks and the way forward. Retrieved from DownToEarth: https://www.downtoearth.org.in/blog/governance/education-for-tribals-bottlenecks-and-the-way-forward-74751
- Trusts, T. (2020). Tribal Education. Retrieved from Tata Trusts: https://www.tatatrusts.org/our-work/education/broadening-access/tribal-education#:
- Upmanyu, M. (2016). The Tribal Education in India, Status, Challenges and Issues. Retrieved from Novelty Journals: https://www.noveltyjournals.com/upload/paper/The%20Tribal%20Education%20in%20India-869.pdf
- Vinu, M. (2021). Tribal education and quality of life: issues & challenges. Retrieved from The International Journal of Indian Psychology
- Basu,D.D. (2013), "Introduction to the Constitution of India", publishers: Gurgaon: LexisNexis.
- Basu, D.D. (2006), "Shorter Constitution of India", publishers: Nagpur: Wadhwa.
- Kashyap, C.Subhas,(2019), "Our Constitution: An Introduction to India's Constitution and Constitutional Law",Publishers : natonal book trust,india.
- Bakshi, P.M.(2006),"The Constitution of India: Selective

Comments",Publishers : Universal law publishing Co.

- Bare Act , (2021),"The Constitution of India", Publishrs : universal Book co.

- MADHAVI POTHUKUCHI, Birsa Munda — freedom fighter 'Dharti Abba' who championed tribal rights,The Print,https://theprint.in/theprint-profile/birsa-munda-freedom-fighter-dharti-abba-who-championed-tribal-rights/321466/,2019.

- ARFA JAVAIDBirsa Munda: All you need to know about the tribal freedom fighter,Jagran Josh,

- https://www.jagranjosh.com/general-knowledge/birsa-munda-1591683253-1, 2020

- Sargana,Tribute to the Indian tribal freedom fighter Birsa Munda,Akhil Bharatiya Vidyarthi Parishad,https://www.abvp.org/news/tribute-indian-tribal-freedom-fighter-birsa-munda,2020

- Anupa Kujur, Birsa Munda, spearhead of tribal fight against British,DECCAN HERAlD,https://www.deccanherald.com/national/birsa-munda-spearhead-of-tribal-fight-against-british-776510.html,2019

- Birsa Munda, Wikipedia, the free encyclopedia, https://en.wikipedia.org/wiki/Birsa_Munda

- Akula, S. (2013). Education for Children of Tribal Community- A Study of Adilabad District. *American International Journal of Research in Humanities, Arts and Social Sciences*, 4(2), 192-196. Retrieved from http://iasir.net/AIJRHASSpapers/AIJRHASS13-377.pdf

- Andrabi, A. A. & Jabeen, N. (2018). Scheduled Tribes Education in India: Issues and Challenges. *Scholarly Research Journal for Interdisciplinary Studies*, 5(45), 10738-10747. Retrieved from http://www.srjis.com/pages/pdfFiles/15337177379.%20Dr.%20Azad%20Ahmad%20Andrabi.pdf

- Arya, S. & Chauhan, T. (2012). A critical study of tribal education: with special reference to women's. Retrieved from https://www.researchgate.net/publication

- Basumatary, M. (2020). The issue, Challenge, and Development Problems in Socio, Economic, and Culture of Tribal People in Assam. *International Journal of Recent Technology and Engineering*, 8(5), 5222-5224. Retrieved from https://www.ijrte.org/wp-content/uploads/papers/v8i5/D9226118419.pdf

- Daripa, S. K. (2017). Tribal Education in India: Government Initiative and Challenges. *International Journal of Research in Social Sciences.* *7*(10), 156-166. Retrieved from https://www.ijmra.us/project%20doc/2017/IJRSS_OCTOBER2017/IJMRA-12325.pdf

- Kapur, R. (2019). Problems in Tribal Education. Retrieved from https://www.researchgate.net/publication/334479483_Problems_in_Tribal_Education/link/5d2d805d299bf1547cb9e43c/download
- Mukherjee, A. (2009). Tribal Education in India: An Examination of Cultural Imposition and Inequality. (MA Thesis, Kansas State University Manhattan, Kansas). Retrieved from https://krex.k-state.edu/dspace/bitstream/handle/2097/1520/AnirbanMukherjee2009.pdf?sequence=1&isAllowed=y
- Sahu, K. K. (2014). Challenging Issues of Tribal Education in India. *IOSR Journal of Economics and Finance*, *3*(2), 48-52. Retrieved from https://www.iosrjournals.org/iosr-jef/papers/vol3-issue2/Version-2/J03224852.pdf
- Sahu, K. K. (2014). Myths and Realities of Tribal Education: A Primary Study in Similipal Area of Odisha. *International Journal of Humanities and Social Science Invention*, *3*(4), 1-6. Retrieved from http://www.ijhssi.org/papers/v3(4)/Version-1/A03410106.pdf
- Satyasavitri, V. B. & Honakeri, P. M. (2018). Impact of Ashram Schools Issues and Challenges of Tribal Education in India. *International Journal of Scientific and Research Publications*, 8(2), 475-478. Retrieved from http://www.ijsrp.org/research-paper-0218/ijsrp-p7459.pdf
- Sujatha, K. (n.d.). Education Among Scheduled Tribes. Retrieved from http://www.doccentre.net/docsweb/Education/Scanned_material/analysis_Tribals.pdf
- https://indiaeducationdiary.in/literacy-among-tribal-girls-and-women-an-overview
- https://journalsofindia.com/tribals-and-tribal-policy/
- http://inet.vidyasagar.ac.in:8080/jspui/bitstream/123456789/5346/11/11_ch._2._evolution_of_Tribal_Policy_in_India.pdf
- https://www.culturalsurvival.org/publications/cultural-survival-quarterly/tribal-education-india
- https://www.indiatoday.in/education-today/featurephilia/story/tribal-education-and-its-challenging-issues-in-india-965832-2017-03-16z
- https://www.thehindu.com/news/national/pm-modi-